3- BOOK SERIES
"QUANTUM CRISIS"

Best Selling Author of
Quantum Crisis-II and Quantum Crisis-III

RAJ D. RAJPAL
B.Sc.(Honors), D.A.P.R., D.M., D.C.S., D.M., M.B.A. (Ohio)

QUANTUM CRISIS-I

QUANTUM CRISIS-I
ORIGIN OF GLOBAL FINANCIAL CRISES

ISBN : 978-0-9783550-3-6

Best Selling Author of
Quantum Crisis-II and Quantum Crisis-III

Best Selling Author of
Quantum Crisis-I and Quantum Crisis-III

RAJ D. RAJPAL
B.Sc.(Honors), D.A.P.R., D.M., D.C.S., D.M., M.B.A. (Ohio)

QUANTUM CRISIS-II

QUANTUM CRISIS-II
THE GREAT FINANCIAL & CREDIT CRISIS
2007 - 2009

ISBN : 978-0-9783550-4-3

Best Selling Author of
Quantum Crisis-I and Quantum Crisis-III

Best Selling Author of
Quantum Crisis-I and Quantum Crisis-II

RAJ D. RAJPAL
B.Sc.(Honors), D.A.P.R., D.M., D.C.S., D.M., M.B.A. (Ohio)

QUANTUM CRISIS-III

QUANTUM CRISIS-III
WINNING INVESTMENT STRATEGIES
TO PROSPER THROUGH
THE GLOBAL FINANCIAL AND CREDIT CRISIS

ISBN : 978-0-9783550-5-0

Best Selling Author of
Quantum Crisis-I and Quantum Crisis-II

AUTHOR SUGGESTS YOU READ ALL THREE BOOKS
SEQUENTIALLY FOR FULL UNDERSTANDING OF
GLOBAL FINANCIAL & CREDIT CRISIS

QUANTUM CRISIS III
-WINNING INVESTMENT STRATEGIES TO PROSPER THROUGH THE GLOBAL FINANCIAL AND CREDIT CRISIS

By

RAJ D.RAJPAL

B.Sc. (Honors), G.C.E. (Cambridge), D.A.P.R., D.M., D.C.S., D.P.S., M.B.A (Ohio)

BEST-SELLING AUTHOR OF:
QUANTUM CRISIS 1: THE ORIGIN OF FINANCIAL CRISES
&
QUANTUM CRISIS 2: THE GREAT FINANCIAL & CREDIT CRISIS
2007-2009
More info at: www.pioneer-communication.com

PIONEER COMMUNICATION PUBLISHERS
BOOKS BOUTIQUE

FINANCE SERIES
QUANTUM CRISIS 1
QUANTUM CRISIS 2
QUANTUM CRISIS 3
OFFSHORE INVESTMENTS: THE MILLIONAIRE VISION
OFFSHORE HAVENS: THE FOUR BEST-KEPT SECRETS OF MILLIONAIRES

SALES AND MARKETING SERIES
QUANTUM SELLING
QUANTUM SALES MANAGEMENT
QUANTUM MARKETING

MANAGEMENT SERIES
QUANTUM ETHICS

SELF-IMPROVEMENT SERIES
QUANTUM PUBLIC SPEAKING
YOU HAVE IT ALL NOW: YOUR LIFE IS TRULY YOURS TO DISCOVER & ENJOY

OTHER FORTHCOMING BOOKS
UNCONDITIONAL LOVE
UNCONDITIONAL YOGA
UNCONDITIONAL HEALTH
UNCONDITIONAL WEALTH
UNCONDITIONAL HEALING
UNCONDITIONAL SPIRITUALITY
UNCONDITIONAL WEIGHT LOSS

QUANTUM CRISIS III
-WINNING INVESTMENT STRATEGIES TO PROSPER THROUGH THE 2007-09 GLOBAL FINANCIAL AND CREDIT CRISIS

By

RAJ D.RAJPAL

B.Sc. (Honors), D.A.P.R., D.M., D.C.S. (U.S.), D.P.S., M.B.A. (Ohio)

National Quality Award Winner
Sales Coach and Public Speaker
Trainer, Bob Proctor Basic Program, Canada
Sales Trainer, Counselor Selling Program, U.S.A.
Diploma, Graduate Marketing Management Program.
Trophy Winner, Public Speaking, Indo-American Society.
Provisional Applicant, Million Dollar Round Table, U.S.A.
Diploma, Graduate Advertising & Public Relations Program.
Uni-Lever Gold Medal Recipient-Graduate Marketing Management
Trainer, Bob Proctor Advanced Motivation Series Program, Canada.

PIONEER COMMUNICATION
www.pioneer-communication.com

PUBLISHER:
PIONEER COMMUNICATION, CANADA

Orders for additional books can be placed directly at:
rdrajpal@yahoo.com
National Library of Canada
Rajpal Raj D., 1951–
Quantum Crisis/Raj D. Rajpal
Includes Index
ISBN: 978-0-9783550-5-0

This book is dedicated to the understanding of the serious challenges facing us--- as we set out to conquer this great global financial and credit crisis.

Awareness, understanding and meaningful investor actions are required in addition to total integration of personal, financial and spiritual priorities. This will help protect both one's inner peace and external wealth while guaranteeing a more sane and profitable future for our children.

TABLE OF CONTENTS

CHAPTER 6

THE SECOND PILLAR OF YOUR FINANCIAL FOUNDATION:
INVESTMENTS

LEARN TO INVEST--- SIMPLE LESSONS IN INVESTING
MASLOW'S MODEL OF HUMAN NEEDS
RAJPAL INVESTMENT SUITABILITY PYRAMID

CHAPTER 7

THE THIRD PILLAR OF YOUR FINANCIAL FOUNDATION:
RISK MANAGEMENT

LEARN TO PROTECT:
YOUR LOVED ONES
YOUR BUSINESS
YOUR RETIREMENT INCOME NEEDS
YOUR CHILDREN'S EDUCATION NEEDS
YOUR WEALTH IN EVENT OF DISABILITY

CHAPTER 8

THE FOURTH PILLAR OF YOUR FINANCIAL FOUNDATION:
EFFECTIVE TAX MANAGEMENT OF YOUR RESOURCES

DIRECT VISIBLE TAXES
INDIRECT & SOMETIMES HIDDEN TAXES
OTHER TAXES
SIMPLIFIED ASSET PROTECTION CONCEPTS

CHAPTER 13
PLANNING & PROTECTING AGAINST FUTURE THREATS TO YOUR FINANCIAL SECURITY
THREAT OF MARRIAGE BREAKDOWN—PRE/POST NUPTIAL AGREEMENT
THREAT OF BUSINESS PARTNER CONFLICT------
CHALLENGE OF PROPERLY DRAFTED PARTNERSHIP AGREEMENT
THREAT OF ALL OTHER POTENTIAL LITIGATION---
LIABILITY COVERAGE REQUIREMENTS
BANKRUPTCY THREAT—SETTING EFFECTIVE FINANCIAL AND LEGAL STRUCTURES PRIOR TO BANKRUPTCY

SECTION 2
ADVANCED INVESTMENT TECHNIQUES

CHAPTER 14
OVERALL RISK MANAGEMENT STRATEGY FOR THE ORDINARY INVESTOR
WHAT IS RISK MANAGEMENT
UNDERSTANDING OF LIFE, DISABILITY,
GROUP AND HEALTH INSURANCE

CHAPTER 15
INVESTMENT/ASSET ALLOCATION STRATEGIES
FOR THE SMART INVESTOR

CHAPTER 16
SUPERCHARGING YOUR RETIREMENT STRATEGY

SECTION 3
PERSONAL GROWTH STRATEGIES FOR WEALTH ACCELERATION

SUMMARY OF ILLUSTRATIONS

ILLUSTRATION 1
PIGGY BANK

ILLUSTRATION 2
MASLOW'S MODEL –HIERARCHY OF HUMAN NEEDS

ILLUSTRATION 3
RAJPAL INVESTMENT SUITABILITY PYRAMID©

ILLUSTRATION 4A
INVESTOR– INSURANCE COMPANY RELATIONSHIP

ILLUSTRATION 4B
LIST OF INVESTOR CONTINGENCIES

ILLUSTRATION 4C
LIST OF CONTINGENCIES (CONTINUED)

ILLUSTRATION 5
SAMPLE BUY–SELL PARTNERSHIP AGREEMENT
FUNDED BY LIFE INSURANCE

PREFACE

2007 was a particularly challenging year for most investors. What started as a faint Headwind developed into a massive hurricane of unbelievable strength. The speed and impact of this financial hurricane was unprecedented in modern history.

October 2007 marked the beginnings of this financial hurricane. The impact of this unbelievably vital and destructive headwind was felt all over the world. The first manifestation of this devastation was felt intimately in the country, which represented the epicenter of this crisis---- the United States of America. The US stock market price values reflected the early symptoms of this larger financial malaise. In October 2007 it swung up and down ---- but the general trend was downwards. Stock prices depreciated expeditiously-----and this deep downward price decline spread to bond and commodity contracts too. Commodities, which were always thought to be a great hedge against future inflation, also saw precipitous drops in value. Nothing seemed safe anymore. All markets simultaneously tanked----- it was an unbelievable sell off. And, to add misery to madness, the Federal Reserve continued its path to lower interest rates, simultaneously decimating investors' interest savings and retirement returns for the older segment of the population. All of a sudden nothing was safe anymore. All the financial advisors and their advice were not worth a dime.

In the backdrop of this vast destruction of investor and public wealth, was a notion in my mind that this was a subject worth investigating. I visualized myself being in a position to practically and positively assist a common investor in understanding and resolving these current and future financial risks. Looking at my over two decades of experience in risk management, I took upon myself the challenge to write a book which would, for the first time explain to the public the history, causes and effects of this financial tsunami. But to be valuable book, I would then have a continuing obligation and responsibility to present valid risk management initiatives to the personal investor with an end view of developing strategies to protect such investor's nest egg----- irrespective of whether this nest egg was a modest sum of money in a bank account or a multimillion dollar estate.

With these thoughts and feelings, I started this project of writing this monumental thesis. This book is more than sixty chapters long (counting present and future editions to this book).

The author humbly submits that an understanding of the causes and effects and practical action steps by an investor to mitigate such astronomic risks will go a long way to protect and enhance your life savings and life values.

May this book assist you in accomplishing such objectives.

INTRODUCTION

This book's history starts in the United States. Where it ends is anyone's guess. But to be absolutely candid and forthright, the entire blame for this crisis rests in the hands of the most powerful country in the world--- the United States of America. Since this country marks the very epicenter of this financial earthquake, it is important to start the story with the goings on financially in this part of the Western World. This book therefore focuses greatly on this epicenter. How quickly we resolve this global financial and credit problem will rest on how well the financial repair is conducted in the United States.

The great financial and credit crisis of 2007-2009 amplified itself when greedy banks, insurance companies and other financial intermediaries/institutions (within the massive financial system) decided to systematically exploit the opportunities available to them. This was done with a view to maximize their profits with no consideration of what impact such profits would have on the global financial system.

At this time of our financial histories in the US, interest rates were very low----- this encouraged risk-taking by ordinary investors and speculators alike. With a negative real rate of borrowing, financial institutions lent billions of dollars out. This money landed up in everyone's hands. Such money was being invested in the ever-expanding real estate market as investors purchased homes and commercial properties with little or no money down (with very few credit restrictions).

This upward demand for real estate resulted in real estate prices hitting the roof nationally. Along with this investment behavior was the accompanying actions of investors to speculate in the stock and commodity markets. This resulted in ever increasing prices of everything from homes to office buildings to stock prices. The unlimited amount of capital available in the marketplace was largely due to a financial innovation called "SECURITIZATION." Securitization was the magic financial engineering concept and technique, which assisted such financial institutions in creating and transporting these massive amounts of risk to third parties. By employment of the securitization process, banks, as one example, transferred their credit risks of lending money to third parties. In this process, banks were ably assisted by their evil counterparts in the investment banking system. The investment banks packaged and repackaged such bank loans into securities and sold them to different banks and investors all over the world. This is how an American problem became an international financial problem with "toxic assets" infecting all countries in the world and decimating global bank balance sheets. Let us try to understand the securitization process a bit better since this can be traced to the real roots of this financial and credit crisis. Securitization is a process where ordinary banks would resell their loans to investment banks, which then packaged them into loans of different tranches/qualities. Tranche 1, for example, could be loans made to individuals with good credit.

Tranche 2 were loans to individuals with average credit while Tranche 3 were loans made to questionable credit risks, like sub-prime borrowers.

Using this financial process banks were able to offload their loans to third parties. The third party would make an investment based on its risk-return requirement. If it wanted to earn a higher return it would invest in Tranche 2 as compared to Tranche 1.

As loan growth exploded in the US, more and more people were being allowed to borrow money to buy houses, which they could never afford (to pay back) by fraudulent banks and mortgage brokers. But this process of upward moving house prices could not go on forever. When the subprime borrowers started defaulting on their loan obligations, this started the process of collapse of the credit markets. There was so much money floating around and no investor really knew what any lenders portfolio was worth. This created confusion and finally panic in the marketplace. Where was one to invest? How would one know if one would get their money back after investing in say, a bank or other financial institution? Frankly, no one knew, because the toxic assets were neatly distributed in different parts of the financial system. Also no financial institution was willing to come clean on their real exposure to toxic assets. We got into an environment where everything was suspect. This resulted in the extreme stand by banks, which stopped trusting each other. Even for one bank to lend to another overnight became a problem. This started the credit crisis.

Since banks stopped or restricted lending, businesses could not get loans to continue their activities--- this resulted in them laying off workers, who now stopped spending money since they had less of it. The crisis had run a full circle. Easy lending, lots of money around, speculation and growth of asset markets followed with distrust, lack of confidence and a credit crisis. This resulted in job layoffs, lower consumer spending and a general lack of investor confidence. And the bottom line was that this crisis was impacting what hurts most, which is an average individual's ability to earn (as a result of a lost job) and his accompanying inability to spend. When you looked at the effect of this crisis on a macro-level, it invariably lead to economic disruption and downturn accompanied with a higher national unemployment rate, lack of consumer confidence and lower production of Gross National Product.

Many factors lead to this crisis. Inefficient and ineffective bank supervision, too lax an interest rate policy by the Federal Reserve and the massive securitization of loans by investment banks and regular banks all hand a hand in this crisis.

This book will slowly but surely take you through all the historical and actual steps in this evolving crisis. In the process, it will give you a bird's eye view of the problem and a 360-degree understanding of the crisis. It will then move forward to discuss policy prescriptions and most importantly look at what you can as a private investor do to protect and grow your nest egg.

21

This introduction serves to preview what is going to follow in his book. Read on--- the book is interesting and lively. May this presentation assist you in living a better financial and personal life and protect your hard earned assets.

CHAPTER 1

MISSION STATEMENT

The purpose of this three-book series (Quantum Crisis 1, Quantum Crisis II and Quantum Crisis III) is unique in the sense that it tries to understand the whole picture reflecting the universal financial and credit crisis. This particular crisis is like no other since the Great Depression and therefore needs patient and clear understanding. The problems surrounding this crisis are very complex---- causes of this crisis which appear like simple concepts presented by the media and other vested interests do not reflect the fundamental reasons triggering this problem. There are numerous causes, some which appear on the surface and others more subliminal. In fact, it is the dangerous combination of a variety of lethal causes all acting at the same time, which has precipitated this crisis.

The book revolves around three different time curtains representing the past ("Quantum Crisis 1" Book), the present ("Quantum Crisis II" Book) and the future ("Quantum Crisis III" Book). "Quantum Crisis 1" talks about what money represents and how and where it derives its power and influence from. This part continues as a historical journey into how money was created and what shape and form it appears in the present. "Quantum Crisis I" goes into the past history of bubbles, depressions and public mania.

This history is critical in understanding what has happened in the past and how the string of past, present and future events are interlinked.

In this process, the reader understands that "financial crises" existed through many past centuries in almost every country in the world. Causes of the prominent crises are then elucidated with a moral or policy prescription at the end of each historical crises point. It is surprising that wise economists, financial institutions and representative governments have still not learnt to spot these irrational exuberances in advance----- nor have they learnt to set up effective risk management and risk mitigation systems to control such negative wealth destruction occurrences.

"Quantum Crisis II" explains what went wrong with the current global financial and credit crisis and what we can do to solve this problem immediately with the least amount of pain.

"Quantum Crisis III" goes to the most important part of this 3-book series---- which is, what you, as an ordinary investor can do to protect and build your nest egg. It is not enough to know and understand this crisis. What is critical at this stage is to apply this newfound knowledge to grow your wealth and guarantee your lifestyle for generations to come.

In short the mission statement is part history, part an understanding of current problems with the second half discussing causes and policy prescriptions to solve this problem in addition to preventing such financial catastrophes in the future.

And the last part talks about the most important person in the world--- which is, of course YOU with all the financial challenges you must now face as you struggle to protect and grow your wealth.

In closing, the mission statement is to educate, enlighten and grow your understanding of the financial world in a straight, plain and factual manner. May this mission statement serve to protect you in every shape and form conceivable.

CHAPTER 2

PHILOSOPHY BEHIND A CRISIS

Times have indeed changed today. The global crisis in front of us has fundamentally changed the nature of our relationships with each other. In times of plenty and prosperity when no thought was given to money, people lived in nice homes and had secure jobs. The family looked forward to two vacations, one in the summer and one around Christmas. When money was not immediately available there was the reliable credit card, which could stave off any scarcities. While all of this was happening, inflation was generally controllable and there was always enough to spend in spite of the daily increases in the cost of living. And our marvelous home, the ultimate bastion of free enterprise would quietly go up in value every year. Everything was fine and dandy. This was until the global financial crisis hit home. And hit home it did and the effect was a very severe jolt into reality.

The first manifestations of the crisis were the plunging values of homes in most neighborhoods. In early 2005 the deceleration had started in the United States--- first with slight drops till suddenly home prices started decreasing exponentially. The final housing shock arrived sometime in 2008 when the mortgage on the home was greater than its market value ------this provided a homeowner with his first glimpse with scarcity and poverty. Still things were going along fine till the stock market tanked in 2008.

And October 2008 was like no other month or year. At around this time the US Government refused to bailout the investment banking firm, Bear Stearns, and everything went downhill subsequent to that. 2009 was a time of increased change as national consumer confidence plummeted and the US started losing jobs in the first two months of the year at a rate in excess of 500,000 jobs per month. Now, you had zero or inappreciable equity in your home, your stock market portfolio had tanked by over 50% and you either had or were in danger of losing your job. Suddenly there was a real crisis–––– it was a personal crisis of unbelievable portions and the only story out there was one of personal survival.

This crisis changed in many ways the relationship between people. Everyone was so self-consumed in his or her financial and life issues that there was very little time for retrospection of the wider issues, which had created this problem. One of such issues was the relationship between the people and the global financial system. Did the controllers/primary players in the financial system have the right to decimate individual wealth? And how much greed (on their part) was enough? And now that the destruction was complete who would save us? America, which had always believed in the free enterprise system where the markets would sort out what is right and return to equilibrium suddenly realized that this business model, was ineffective and inefficient in solving the massive new financial problems.

Suddenly the Government had to sort out the mess to redistribute resources so that the problem could be solved and resources could be properly allocated among the different players in the financial system. And what about the financial architecture surrounding the financial system? Something was seriously wrong here too in a way where a few powerful constituents like global banks, investment banks, insurance companies and mortgage related entities proved that in the name of greed they had the power to destroy the otherwise worthwhile financial architecture?

The philosophy behind this crisis starts with a self-examination on the part of all components of this global financial system to understand their individual roles and effects and to design proper systems to insure stability and prosperity to everyone. As the financial crisis developed, it showed how few powerful constituents could destroy the lifestyle of billions of people worldwide.

The philosophy behind the crisis needed to deal with human values---- the basic values of self-respect, concern about other individual's rights and a desire to work cooperatively and peacefully knowing there was enough for everyone. The current crisis brought to the fore several ethical issues that expressed them in the total callousness and indifference of some financial players to the detriment and ruin of hundreds of small and medium sized players. And this abuse of ethics involved primarily the large financial organizations like the commercial and super powerful investment banks along with their brethren in insurance and mortgage companies.

Such large corporations in the United States (predominantly) violated the rights of everyone else to survive and prosper and given the interrelatedness of the global financial system such unconscionable and criminal behavior resulted in people suffering all over the world. All of a sudden there were 20 million people out of work (in early 2009) in China due to reduced global demand for their products in addition to millions of people displaced in Asia, Europe and Australia people who due to no fault of their own had become indirect negative beneficiaries of the global financial scam perpetrated by a few super large financial institutions in the United States.

Looking at this massive and catastrophic effect on individual's lives---- this destruction and suffering point to a time which has now come for the world to become one. By this I mean, there is a great and extreme need for humans to work co-operatively and peacefully in every field of endeavor. Globalization has become the first step, which has brought people and cultures in intimate contact with each other---- this has all started with a need to serve the needs of international business. However this movement is only the beginning.

The philosophy of good business ethics is intimately connected with this need for companies and individuals to honestly talk with one another. What invariably gets in the way of clear, honest communication is the presence of diversity of language and cultural backgrounds of all such parties to such conversation.

Also one has to be cognizant of the motivating factors behind such conversations, whether such purpose is to do business together or to understand each other better, religiously, physically and/or spiritually.

When we look at the state of ethics in this world, one cannot hide the fact that there is at every level and corner of this world a sense of disarray and disrepair caused by ceaselessly selfish acts of both individuals and groups. Let me explain. In order for us to grow together we need to be aware and alert of each other's needs. Only when such understanding is crystal clear can we hope to proceed with the arduous and challenging task of optimally relating to each other. Unfortunately, what is actually happening in the world is the reverse of this ideal process of communication. The individual, corporation or nation first thinks of all it priorities and then works out a way of relating with the other individual, corporation or nation. Therefore, there is no proper communication or relationship. The more powerful nation or corporation gets the upper hand in such relationships. The world as we see it now is in a constant state of war between the strong and the weak. The strong represent the haves of this world; the weak represent the have-nots. The stronger, more financially capitalized and agile company tends to dominate world markets and creates disharmonious relationships with its customers and the world at large. Surely, when Green Peace and other world- minded individuals and organizations protest at G-7 meetings, these protests represent some cause and reason.

I am not a member of the Green Peace organization nor do I belong to any other activist groups. But I know one thing for sure and that is the fact that the time has come when big and small nations, big and small corporations and corporations and lawmakers sit down and do something to clean up the mess. And what is this mess? It is the mess of unbridled exploitation of energy and financial resources. It is the filthy and unconscionable act of throwing up greenhouse gases to make a profit at any cost. It is actions made by groups of executives to rip off the public by financial misrepresentations and distortions. This nonsense needs to stop right now.

Although what is happening now ethically is very negative we must realize that even this cloud has a silver lining. Maybe the Lord has wanted all this to happen to bring us all together in a spirit of compromise, adjustment and peace.

The philosophy behind a global crisis points to a deeper and honest understanding of all the problems being created today as a result of a lack of concern for others. This philosophy also calls for all parties responsible for such "pollution" to sit together and talk earnestly with a view to solving such problems immediately and instantaneously. Corporations must talk to their customers, nations must talk with other nations, and people must talk with other people to overcome cultural gaps. We must all try hard to communicate and act together to save the world. This is not a Utopian vision. It is the truth. The World is decaying and dying slowly but surely. But this is not the end of Life or Existence.

We need to step back and look at the problems we have created and come back with a humble positive mind to undo all the wrongs of the past. This is absolutely possible given the depth and breadth of human intelligence. We have had the power to advance technologically; to send a man to the moon; to create numerous and marvelous scientific advancements and even to prolong life itself. Why can the human mind not go one step forward and solve this bigger problem it has created through poor communications and deplorable personal and business ethics?

In the solution to this problem lies our philosophical and real advancement. And the message is simple. To live together in this marvelous and wonderful world, we must understand why we seek to dominate others, why we seek to use unethical actions as an excuse to get ahead in our lives and how we can come together and all win together by respecting everyone's right to live, whether it is a poor man living in a slum in India or an African afflicted with AIDS.

The burning need today is for the human to work together with his fellow human to bring about good in the world. Good ethics, good conduct and proper action always starts and ends with the human being. Are we really ready to make this great inner change? On the answer to this question lies the hope and salvation of Mankind.

Work together honestly, help others and co-operate harmoniously and the World will always be there to supply all our needs.

Keep fighting and building walls, misrepresent constantly, continue expressing unethical behavior and feed greenhouse gases to the atmosphere and our world will cease to exist, as we know it. The choice is yours.

It is the author's fervent prayer, that we can make decisive and positive change at the individual, corporate and national level to make this world a better place for our children and us.

May this book be a small opening to get us into the vast expanse of universal consciousness, where everything is possible.

CHAPTER 3
PSYCHOLOGY OF A CRISIS

The current global financial and credit crisis had its intimate roots in the manifestation of human greed. How else can you explain the massive fraud, misrepresentation and cruel exploitation of financial players in the worldwide system? This greed was amplified by the superiority and secrecy of prevailing knowledge. Let me explain. Firstly, we need to put the blame where it is due. The blame primarily rests in the hands of the large US commercial and investment banks, along with other influential mega players, like US hedge funds, the US insurance leadership under AIG Insurance and US mortgage related outfits like mortgage brokers, mortgage originators, mortgage re-sellers, and etcetera.

These large players engaged in severe and unconscionable gambling on an unprecedented scale. Their investment behavior had all the hallmarks of engaging in activities with unlimited upside potential and no downside investment risk. The commercial banks that sold home loans to the investment bank for further sale had no risk. They took the loan off their balance sheet the moment they sold it to the investment banks. There was zero risk for them. In an environment of low interest rates and rising home prices and availability of capital they lent billions of dollars to sub-prime borrowers, and immediately resold these loans to investment banks after making a substantial profit.

The investment banks then repackaged the loans into different Tranches (credit tranches) and sold it to institutional investors, foreign governments, and foreign banks through the mechanism of direct sales. They also had no skin in the game and could engage in shifting billions of dollars of risk all over the world. The differentiating factor for these investment package sales and what made them easily saleable was the paucity of information. This paucity of information was created by the employment of advanced financial engineering techniques. The securitization process was so complicated and devious that no one, save the investment banks themselves, knew exactly what was inside these loans. In such absence of information the investment community surrendered their collective intelligence and judgment to the well known US rating agencies. They believed that these rating agencies had exercised due diligence in analyzing and assessing the risk worthiness of these tranches of sub-prime and other mortgage loans. But the rating agencies themselves failed to exercise financial prudence in evaluating the appropriate risk of these investment vehicles. Such rating agencies erroneously labeled most of these real estate loans, packaged collaterized loans and other asset-backed mortgages as AAA never anticipating in their mathematical valuation models that the real estate market would show such significant downward correction. Huge banks and institutions all over the world bought these securities trusting the declared risk ratings provided.

However and very mysteriously none of these sophisticated investors paid attention to the inherent conflict of interest between the rating agencies and issuers of debt (which was being evaluated by the agencies). The non-palatable fact was that the that the issuers of debt like investment banks paid these rating organizations for their services---- one wonders how and why most of these securities were labeled AAA.

The financial crisis became serious when investors had no way of determining where the toxic assets were and therefore could not professionally value any specific investment. Since the toxic assets were everywhere, there was an immediate loss of investor confidence causing a lack of trust and confidence in the market. This led to the credit crisis and the deplorable market condition today.

Another important psychological factor, which involved the manipulation of other financial investors by these large banks and insurance companies basically, revolves around the issue of ethics. These large players exhibited very poor ethics in their business dealings with others as they decided to maximize profit at any cost with no regard to the values and needs of others.

Therefore, greed, a superiority based on having exclusive and protected knowledge about loans securitization (knowledge which the investment public did not have), and a poor sense of ethics all contributed to this financial mess the world is in now.

Let us now turn our attention to the issues surrounding the need for proper ethical behavior on part of these large financial institutions.

To understand ethical behavior one needs to look closely at human psychology. Human psychology is a fascinating subject. How and why we act and the results there from can fill thousands and thousands of pages of psychological material. Looking at our psychology in terms of ethics, we must first step in and understand our motivation factors. Abraham Maslow, a psychologist I respect a great deal, came up with a hierarchy of human needs pyramid. He believed that every action we took had its roots in our quest to fulfill a dominant need or desire. However, we tended to focus on first fulfilling basic needs, like the need for food, water and shelter. After we achieved this, we moved on to our safety and physiological needs. Then we spent our energy in meeting with our self-esteem needs and so on........

What does an understanding of Maslow's hierarchy of needs have to do with the psychology of ethics? I believe it has a lot to do with a deeper understanding of this subject matter. Depending on which part of the world you live in and your current economic and political situation, you may be forced to behave in certain ways. If you live in India in a slum, your day-to-day life may involve struggling to get enough bread, water and salt for your family. With a lack of abundant jobs in your community accompanied by the ever-increasing financial demands from your family, you may be forced to lie, cheat and steal to survive.

On the other hand, if you live in the vast profitable expanse of North America, you may not have the same sense of economic urgencies as a poor Indian.

You probably are paying for a home and have a decent job and worthwhile material comforts. What causes you to lie and cheat and steal?

Coming back to Maslow's pyramid, you are probably attempting to fulfill your needs and desire to get rich quicker than at your usual normal pace. This invariably is what happened to the executives who went to jail when associated with Enron Corporation in the US. These executives were rich; they enjoyed positions of power and influence. However, that was not enough for them. In order to get richer faster they took shortcuts. However, these shortcuts created end results, which were devastating to the lives of thousands of employees at Enron Corporation. Many of these employees lost their entire jobs and life savings and retirement pensions.

So, if you live in a developed economy, you may decide to cheat, lie and steal to get up the corporate ladder faster or to make a fast buck period... There is no other motivating factor to be unethical here.

How do we change this human psychology of survival in India and other developing economies and the preponderance of greed in North America, Europe and most of the developed world??

This is a very difficult question to answer. And in the proper answer and implementation of such answer lies the solution to the ethical dilemmas all around this world.

In order to stem and control the ethical issues, a host of national and international regulations have sprung up.

The Sarbanes-Oxley Act in the US was passed into law soon after the Enron scandal. The United Nations has recommended model corporate governance standards after reviewing all the worldwide problems in the corporate ethics field.

Therefore, we have two sides of a coin, both of which can help solve the problem.

Educate the people; make them more aware of what they are doing wrong; present the social penalties for wrongful action [set up a strong judiciary and police system to monitor ethical performance and develop the societal laws to discourage ethical abuse. Bring the citizens into the picture by large page ads. Show them the cost of unethical behavior to their livelihood and to the nation and world at large. Ask them to become whistleblowers, if they notice or suspect unethical activity at any personal, private, business or corporate level. Give them a monetary reward for spotting and reporting on potentially criminal unethical activity. In India, the Income tax department gives a percentage of the department's recovery of unpaid taxes to the ordinary citizen, who spots and reports someone not paying his fair share of taxes. Why can we not make this a model policy on a worldwide scale? Get the common man to report on unethical behavior. Neither government nor the entire United Nations can effectively police this problem with bad ethics on a consistent basis without the aid of the common man.

The solution to the unethical dilemma philosophically is to pull all stops out and get everyone involved in solving the problems.

Successful solution of this problem at a personal, societal, and judicial/police level will result in better allocation of world resources and a more efficient and productive world. Each and every human being has a responsibility to make the world a better place to live in. This is the first step in solving this problem and removing this curse from this world.

In closing, the challenge in solving the global financial and credit crisis is to be able to understand the driving psychological factors behind this problem: unbelievable greed, an information superiority in terms of the development of exotic financial instruments like securitization and a blatant expression and abuse of personal and business ethics.

All these three psychological factors caused the major problem the world is in now.

CHAPTER 4

PSYCHOLOGY OF A CRISIS RE-VISITED

I feel at this juncture that it makes sense to understand what happened and caused this global crisis. A clear understanding of the problems (on a psychological level) should hopefully prevent this type of crisis from re-occurring in the future. As I had indicated in the last chapter the crisis was caused by massive greed, information manipulation and poor ethics by the large financial houses in the United States. On closer examination, greed, which is the predominant cause of this behavior, has a deep and interconnected relationship with ethics. Poor ethics represents itself in the manifestation of greed and therefore I have attached this chapter for perusal, study and discussion. All I am talking about in this chapter is definitions, understanding and expression of both personal and business ethics; it is my hope that this understanding will help governments and other responsible financial authorities in setting up checks and balances in the system to catch irresponsible, fraudulent and unethical behavior so that such a crisis can never reoccur in the future. It is with this understanding that I am paying particular attention to the subjects surrounding personal and business ethics. Let us now move forward to an understanding of both personal and business ethics.

Wikipedia Encyclopedia defines Ethics as, "Ethics is a major branch of philosophy, which encompasses right conduct and good life. It is significantly broader than the common conception of analyzing right and wrong. A central aspect of ethics is 'the good life,' the life worth living or life that is satisfying, which is held by many philosophers to be more important than moral conduct. The major problem is the discovery of the summun bonum, the greatest good."

Some of the core issues in the study of ethics are:

1. Justice
2. Value
3. Right
4. Duty
5. Virtue
6. Equality
7. Freedom
8. Trust
9. Free will
10. Consent
11. Moral responsibility

Now that the Wikipedia definition is established, let us move along with details on the described components of ethics.

1. JUSTICE

Personal ethics involves the application of justice. In your dealings with others, are you following the code of law established in your community?

Are you dealing fairly and justly with your neighbor and friend? In your business relationships involving your customers are you seeking to provide the best behavior in consonance with the legal codes?

2. VALUE

In terms of value, are you offering a product or service, which represents an ultimate storehouse of value? Is the price of the product commensurate with its quality and embedded service promises? In terms of personal relationships with family and friends, is your relationship one, which embodies the application of the highest standard of value?

3. RIGHT

Do your personal and business actions involve doing something, which is generally regarded as being right? Or are your actions in a gray area---- you are acting legally but have exhibited improper moral behavior. You understand that the law expects certain minimum standards of moral behavior, but that you may be in fact doing something legal and yet something immoral (not right).

4. DUTY

In every situation and interaction with others, are you discharging your duty to the relationship fully and wholly, with no regard to the amount of time, attention or energy expended by you in this process?

5. VIRTUE

The best way of expressing the application of virtue is by quoting from the Bible. The Holy Bible: New Revised Standard Version quotes in Galatians 5:22-23: virtue being:

"Love, joy, peace, patience, kindness, generosity, faithfulness, gentleness and self-control."

The central question the reader must ask himself is if he exercising the above virtues in his dealings with others.

6. EQUALITY

In your everyday relationships, do you approach matters respecting other's right to live and think freely? In business matters, where you seek to influence others, are you approaching your customer with a fair and level sense of equality? Or are you trying to exploit the relationship because of your special and unique status, resources and power?

7. FREEDOM

Are your actions conducted in an environment of personal freedom? And are you dealing with others while respecting their freedom to agree or disagree with your proposition?

Do you accept another's option to accept or reject your ideas and proposition, thereby exercising their personal freedom even if this means your idea or acceptance being put at risk?

8. FREE WILL

When interacting with others, are you conducting your affairs armed with complete self- knowledge of your actions and behaviors? Is your conduct a result of an exercise of free will unabated and uninfluenced by peer or pressure groups? Are you doing what you believe is the best possible thing for your loved one, friend or customer? In short, are you exercising free will all the time?

9. CONSENT

In your everyday actions, are you making sure that you take the consent of all affected parties in your relationships? Or are you taking their involvement in the relationship as granted?

10. MORAL RESPONSIBILITY

Are you aware of your moral responsibilities in communications with others? Are you taking the time to understand and study the impact of your behavior and business interactions with others? Are you enhancing someone else's life? Or are you merely ripping them off?

RELATIONSHIPS BETWEEN ETHICS AND MORALS

Coming back to definitions from Wikipedia, the following further clarifications are provided in terms of the relationships between a study of ethics and morals. Further, there is a good definition of personal ethics. Here are the definitions:

"Ethics and morals are respectively akin to theory and practice. Ethics denotes the theory of right action and the greater good, while morals indicate their practice.

Personal ethics signifies a moral code applicable to individuals, while social ethics means moral theory applied to groups. Social ethics can be synonymous with social and political philosophy, in as much as it is the foundation of a good society or state. Ethics is not limited to specific acts and defined moral codes, but encompasses the whole of moral ideals and behaviors, a person's philosophy of life."

ETHICS AND THE WISE GREEK PHILOSOPHERS

Several Greek philosophers, countless centuries back, had a basic awareness of what ethical action was. According to Socrates, knowledge, which had an intimate connection with human life, was the most important type of knowledge.

Socrates propounded the system of " self-knowledge" as the most important knowledge center. Awareness was the key to good self-knowledge. If a person was aware of the impact of his actions on him and the society at large and had the capacity and capability of distinguishing right from wrong, society would comprise of more wiser citizens and less crime would be committed. Happiness and harmony would result as a direct effect of such enlightened awareness and action.

Another great Greek philosopher, Aristotle envisaged a system of ethics under the heading of the term," self-realizationism." What he meant by this term was that all individuals were born with certain specific and unique talents.

If individuals acted according to their built in nature and used their God-given talents, they would be more content and complete. As a result man should live with moderate virtue. This is normally difficult since this implies doing the right thing, to the right person, at the right time, to the proper extent, in the correct fashion, for the right reason.

To close this chapter, an intimate awareness and knowledge of personal ethics is a starting point and foundation for all human relationships. If one can understand and accept these values, then individuals can work together more fairly.

Business relationships will improve as a result and the incidence of exploitation will decrease. Also, if individuals approach their personal lives with such high standards, then ultimately this will result in better family and community relationships. Everything starts and ends with the individual.

To create a lasting and permanent change in the world ethically, the individual will need to take the first steps in understanding and modifying his behavior for the greater social good. He will need to understand that he is linked with his family, community, business and world around him. Good actions at all levels will create stellar relationships at all levels of existence. This will make the community and world a better and more harmonious place to live in---- a world in which people learn to share and celebrate differences and not a world where talent, money and power control future results.

BUSINESS ETHICS

Business Ethics may be defined as, "a form of the art of applied ethics that examines ethical principles and more or ethical problems that can arise in a business environment." Put simply, business ethics has to do with the ethical value of decisions made by businesses in their quest for profits.
Let us now look at the various issues corporations face as they react and interact with all the different people they do business with.

GENERAL ETHICAL CONSIDERATIONS
The following are some of the areas, which create perceptions of unethical or ethical behavior on part of the corporation:
AREA 1
FUNDAMENTAL OBJECTIVES OF BUSINESS
On a very fundamental basis, one needs to ask why the corporation exists in the first place. If we review the Anglo-American model, which is prevalent in the United Kingdom, the United States and Canada, we understand the predominant and primary reason for doing business from the corporation's perspective is to maximize value for their shareholders. If corporations engage and act on this narrow view at the detriment of relationships with all the other stakeholders, like suppliers, customers and competitors, to name a few, then this process of shareholder maximization at the expense of all other interested parties could be generally viewed as unethical behavior.

AREA 2

CONTRIBUTION TO CORPORATE SOCIAL RESPONSIBILITIES

Another way of assessing the quality of ethics in a corporation is to examine their corporate social responsibility mission. If the corporation talks about such responsibilities but never gets off ground zero to take an active interest and involvement in social causes, then this again can be viewed as unethical activity.

AREA 3

INTER-COMPANY RELATIONSHIPS

How companies behave with each other, particularly when they are in neck-to-neck competition defines their ethical role. When a company sees its competitor as getting weak and exercises an aggressive hostile takeover bid or when a corporation pays someone to spy on its competitors (industrial espionage) determines its outlook to business and ethics in general.

AREA 4

POLITICAL CONTRIBUTIONS AND LOBBYING EFFORTS

The extent of political contributions and the capital expended on lobbying for continuation of existing products and addition of new ones provides the ethical flavor of a company. For example, a tobacco company paying a lobbyist in Washington to get generous advertising exposures for cigarettes can be viewed as a highly unethical action.

A) ACCOUNTING INFORMATION ETHICS

Here are some examples of unethical accounting information use.

Creative accounting scams

The behavior of Enron Corporation in the US is a very good example of how hiding liabilities and misreporting income created a massive problem for everyone who was associated with this company. Briberies and kickbacks When corporations bribe government officials in order to seek government contracts, this constitutes anti-competitive behavior and results in misallocation of societal resources. Insider trading refers to an executive or other interested party having information in advance of public knowledge. For example, if a company is going to start selling a new product after receiving governmental approval, a fact which could increase its stock price. The manufacturing vice-president of this company has this information in advance and seeks purchase of his company shares in advance, knowing that once this announcement is made the share price will rocket upwards and he can make a quick profit. This definitely constitutes unethical behavior.

B) HUMAN RESOURCE MANAGEMENT AND UNETHICAL BEHAVIOR

Human resources ethics deals with all relationships between an employer and an employee.

In such relationships, the employer usually has an upper hand. When we view how the corporation is treating its employees, we then get an idea of the extent of ethical or unethical b behavior on part of the corporation. Here are some examples of corporate behavior in this field:

(i) Discrimination issues surrounding age, gender, race, religion, and disabilities among other factors.

(ii) Factors dealing with representation of employees like actions involving union busting, etcetera

(iii) Actions involving infringement of employee privacy without specific permission and authorization by concerned employee like video, Internet and telephone surveillance of employees and drug testing.

(iv) Occupational safety and employee health issues.

C) MARKETING AND SELLING ETHICS

Several issues abound on unethical use of marketing strategies, techniques and plans of action. These areas cover the following:

(i) Price fixing, price discrimination and price skimming

(ii) Unethical marketing strategies like the Ponzi scheme, Spam electronic marketing, pyramid schemes and planned obsolescence techniques.

51

(iii)   Dangerous and unethical advertising content in the form of subliminal advertising and misrepresentation of product properties.

(iv)   Unethical exploitation of children through specially designed advertisements.

(v)   Unethical representation of products and services by salespeople representing a corporation.

D PRODUCTION ETHICS

The ethics of production has to do with the processes used to produce a product and how ethically a corporation engages in such processes. Here are some of the concerns in the production area:

(i)   Defective, addictive and inherently dangerous products and services (like tobacco, alcohol, weapons manufacturing and bungee jumping)

(ii)   Production processes causing industrial waste into our rivers and general environmental pollution through greenhouse gases, etcetera.

(iii)   Problems arising out of new technologies like genetically modified food.

(iv)   The business of product testing ethics such as animal testing of products.

E   INTELLECTUAL PROPERTY ETHICS

Intellectual property rights are intangible in nature. They are concerned with who has the rights to develop an idea.

Here are some areas of concern:
(1) For example, if an author writes a new book and finds most or all his ideas plagiarized, then this constitutes an intellectual property right infringement.
(2) Issues dealing with patent infringement.
(3) Issues dealing with copyright and trademark infringement.

SIGNIFICANCE OF BUSINESS ETHICS

Since most businesses in the world are in corporate form, how such businesses behave and interact becomes crucial. Here are some of the reasons for the importance of the study of business ethics:

1. There is progressively greater power and influence exerted by corporations on the daily lives of people.
2. Big businesses have the potential power to positively assist or negatively destruct the communities they serve.
3. Businesses have the ability to effect the environment and their immediate communities positively or negatively.

4. With greater pressure being exerted by stakeholders like suppliers, other competitors, it becomes real important to understand how and when corporations should respond to such pressures and what constitutes acceptable behavior in this department.

GLOBALIZATION & ITS IMPACT ON BUSINESS ETHICS

When corporations move away from their normal place of doing business into a new territory or country, several new issues come to the forefront. These are basically legal, accountability and cultural issues. Since the legal framework of doing business shifts when one moves from say, a developed nation to a developing economy, what rules of conduct are OK? The country of incorporation rules of the corporation? The rules of the emerging nation, where it seeks to do trade and investments? Who is going to police the business actions of the corporation now? What about cultural issues? How is the corporation to adapt to a totally different cultural expectation surrounding their products or services? And what about accountability issues? Since the corporation does not really report on a daily basis to anyone, and since it does not have to be held accountable on numerous fronts, how does it serve its accountability responsibilities?

Several of these areas are gray areas. By this I mean, there is no definite standard of conduct here. And this is where most of the misunderstandings and mistrust lies for such multinational corporations.

The United Nations, with a view, to setting up some standards for international trade, business and conduct has suggested the achievement of 8 Millennium Development goals by 2015.

On the United Nations website, "www.undp.org", the following goals are listed:

Goal 1: Eradicate extreme poverty and hunger

Goal2: Achieve universal primary education

Goal 3: Promote gender equality and empower women

Goal 4: Reduce child mortality

Goal 5: Improve maternal health

Goal 6: Combat HIV/AIDS, malaria and other diseases

Goal 7: Ensure environmental sustainability

Goal 8: Develop a global partnership for development

Why am I talking about the United Nations goals? And what does this have to do with business ethics? Simply that since corporations are now becoming multinational in character and have the power to gain and profit from exposure to opportunities all over the world that this opportunity also entails a responsibility on their part. If you are taking from the world then you must also give back to it. And what better way to give back than to assist the United Nations fulfills its eight major goals for the world.

Therefore, if corporations are to be seen as truly caring and concerned global players, they must design and execute their strategies with a view to achieving one or more of these eight goals. Merely paying lip service or designing slick website content on their commitment to world issues is not enough. The message to them is: "Put your money where your mouth is. You simply cannot exploit the world masses. Now is the time to pay back for all your profits and success. Prove that you are really a caring corporate citizen".

This is why the corporation's role in helping the UN will go a long way in improving their credibility and enhancing their reputation as a caring, concerned world player.

THE CASE FOR SUSTAINABILITY

Right through the world, time boundaries apart, more and more people are questioning the ethical behavior of corporations as they plunder and rape the natural resources of this world. Corporate ethical standards are now being applied to include the role of the corporation in respecting and nourishing the resources around it. Issues like pollution creation, the dumping of greenhouse gases, the issues surrounding product recyclability are all creating a framework, where a corporation will be forced to work environmentally and ecologically creatively to preserve the natural balance of the world.

The corporation will need to prove that it is indeed a corporate citizen of the world and cares not only for the goal of making profits but also in playing its part in keeping the balance in Earth between companies and their natural environments.

THE TRIPLE BOTTOM LINE INITIATIVE

Triple bottom line is a phrase coined by John Elkington in 1994. It refers to the triple responsibility of a corporation to take care of the 3 P's: People, Planet and Profit. People in this equation refer to the social responsibilities of corporations.

Planet refers to the environmental responsibilities, including the cause of sustainability by companies. Profit represents what most corporations are in business for anyway.

Triple bottom line actions represent a new way of defining a corporation's responsibility. Instead of a corporation merely maximizing revenue for its shareholders, it now is called to contribute equally to a clean and sound ecological environment and to take positive steps to support all stakeholders. A stakeholder refers to anyone, who is effected directly or indirectly by the actions of the firm.

The stakeholder theory suggests that the firm should be used as vehicle for satisfying and coordinating stakeholder interests, instead of solely maximizing shareholders profit.

In real and practical terms these are some of the actions and initiatives to be taken by a firm to satisfy the triple bottom initiative of People, Planet and Profit.

In order to serve the People/Human Capital initiative a firm needs to have fair and beneficial practice towards labor and the community at large.

In order to ably serve the Planet/Natural capital initiative it needs to benefit the natural order as much as possible by conducting a life cycle assessment of all products manufactured.

This is done to calculate the actual and true environmental cost of growth and harvesting of raw materials to manufacture to distribution to eventual disposal by the end user.

All processes to optimize the ecological and environmental impact of production are taking into consideration by such company. In order to serve the profit initiative the corporation must make a real contribution financially and economically to all the markets it serves.

CONCLUSION

The global financial crisis has shown the ruthless and exploitive of large financial institutions and their leaders. To a great extent, these corporations and their senior management stand guilty in violation of most personal and business ethics principles elucidated in this chapter. From Bernard Madoff and his 50 billion dollar Ponzi scheme to defraud investors to a president of an investment bank who invested more than one million dollars on his office furniture, these examples represent the reasons why this global crisis is like no other. And to come out of this mess will require the coordinated and co-operative effort of all world nations and world people. It is simply too big a problem to be solved by any one country or any group of people. Understanding this massive violation of personal and business ethics should provide a guideline to everyone to measure their personal and business behavior according to a higher ethical standard. We are all in this mess and we all need to work together to develop a higher ethical consciousness---- this consciousness and understanding will work wonders to accelerate the solution of the problem.

THIS PAGE IS INTENTIONALLY LEFT BLANK

SECTION 1

FUNDAMENTAL
FINANCIAL PLANNING CONCEPTS

CHAPTER 5

FIRST PILLAR OF YOUR FINANCIAL FOUNDATION – SAVINGS

LEARN TO SAVE FIRST

"Don't talk to me about return on money.
Tell me first where your money is"

Very few of us understand the value of saving money. However, most of us spend hours fantasizing about becoming rich super-fast. We envy others who are richer than us. Yet we somehow don't see or understand the bigger picture of wealth creation and prosperity. We seem to have some unanswered questions, which seem to nag us day and night. Some of these questions are:

"How did the rich get rich?

Can we someday get super-rich?

Is there are any magic formula to wealth?

Is it possible for us to learn to use some simple technique and method to get rich?

Can our lives be filled with prosperity and happiness?

Or is life going to be an endless battle of paying bills and of financial starvation and mediocrity?"

An old Chinese saying goes like this, "A long journey starts with the first step." This saying is meaningful and significant in your quest for financial excellence. Instead of being intimidated with the long-term goal of being a super multi-millionaire why not instead try to start this long journey by controlling what you can control TODAY --- your first step, your first experiment with super-success. It is perhaps easier to start now with a simple positive goal and action plan than it is to build your wealth overnight. Fear and disbelief are natural negators of prosperity. Many of us might look at our bank account now and our horrendous number of financial obligations and wonder whether it is worthwhile to even consider engaging in this long-term journey of wealth building. Or you may be one of those who have attained an enviable level of wealth in your home country and are wondering if it is worthwhile to take a step into the unknown and uncharted world of offshore finance. Whatever your compelling doubts and fears might be, it goes without saying that the first step of your long journey to financial super wealth and freedom starts with savings. I repeat again most emphatically that THE FIRST STEP IS LEARNING TO SAVE.

PIGGY BANK EPISODE

I know a true story of a young boy growing up in an economically developing country.

Illustration 1

PIGGY BANK

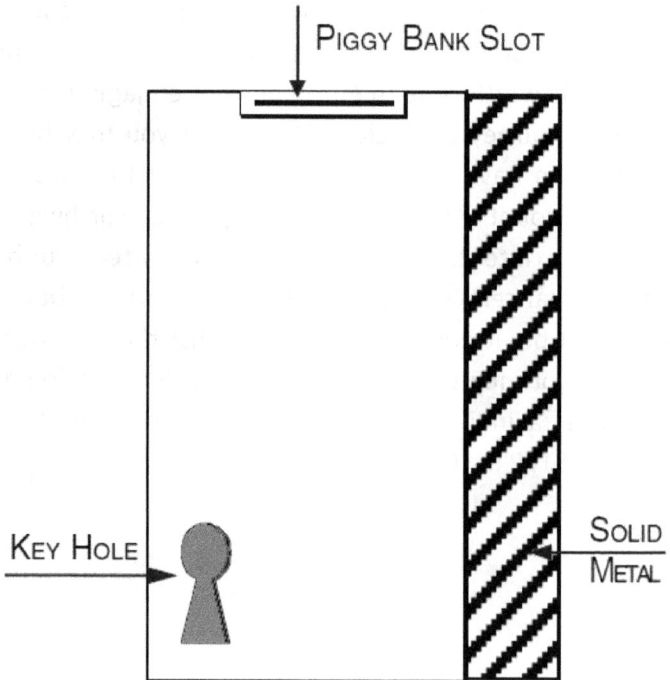

This boy came from a wealthy family. Very early on in his life, this boy's father presented him with a strange looking piggy bank. This was no ordinary piggy bank. For one thing it was shaped like a book in rectangular form. It was made of solid metal. There was only one slot on top. And the piggy bank was always locked. There was no way in the world for the boy to open or remove anything from it. On closer examination of the piggy bank one could see that a special key, which could be inserted in a special slot located in one of the corners locked it. One person --- an official at the Central Bank of India, could only open the piggy bank.

As soon as the piggy bank was totally filled with coins, the kid took it to the bank. The bank official at the Central Bank of India opened the piggy bank in the presence of the 1 child, counted and tabulated the value of the currency coins. The bank official then proceeded to make an entry in the boy's saving passbook and returned the empty piggy bank to the boy. The boy would again start saving small amounts of currency coins, one at a time. When the piggy bank was filled up with coins, he would repeat the process and go back into the bank and have his coins counted, tabulated and credited to his bank savings account. In a few years, the boy accumulated a substantial amount of seed capital.

Where did this kid get his coins? Every time this kid's father sent him out to do some shopping errands he would complete these purchases of different items for his house. It could be a simple errand like buying fresh vegetables from the local market.

Or it might sometimes be supervising some workers who were engaged in some household repair. Whenever his father would give him currency notes to pay the necessary bills, the kid would pay for the allocated expenses, returning only the balance of money left over in currency notes to his father. The kid, though, kept the currency change in coins with him, not returning it to his father. These coins found their way into the piggy bank. His father never took any objection to the kid retaining currency coins, feeling this would encourage the child to save money. And this practice of saving money became a habit with the child. And this taught the child the most valuable lesson in wealth creation --- learning how to save money while at the same time honoring a situation where there was no option to spend it. In this way the capital had a chance to grow gradually over a period of time. In fact, the child had no way of spending the money even if he was tempted to do so. The money had to be returned for entry and bookkeeping purposes to the Bank.

The moral of this story is simple: Anyone can accumulate wealth if one wants to and has a clear crystallized method of saving money. Savings form the first crucial step to wealth creation. But savings must never be touched till a pre-determined goal is achieved.

Also, any accumulated savings must be employed in the future within certain parameters of future investment. This is the only way to build your wealth consistently over a period of time.

Anyone with a burning desire to get rich who follows this method will find himself the proud owner of large amounts of capital. This seed capital will form a foundation on which furthers sums of money can be accumulated giving him a real opportunity to grow wealthy.

THE CANADIAN BANK BOOK EPISODE

In my seminars to financial service professionals in Toronto, Canada I would provide a simple but powerful illustration on the dynamics of saving capital. The concept introduced was that of a distant bank savings account. With respect to these professional's personal investment planning, I would recommend that they open up a savings account in a bank in the closest city away from their home base of operation, Toronto. The only purpose of this bank account would be to accumulate capital unimpeded by any personal or third party demands.

The commitment to be made initially with respect to the operation of this account was that the funds credited to this account would not be touched by the accountholder under any circumstances.

One had to commit that even in the event of a financial crisis or life-threatening emergency that this account would not be touched. No money would ever be withdrawn from this account. The accountholder had to have this die-hard attitude to ensure success of this money-gathering scheme.

Other details with respect to this account would be that it would be a straightforward savings account with no attendant or linked checking account facilities, no attendant or linked debit cards/credit cards/automatic teller machine cards. (ATM's). The bank accountholder would send remittances to such account by mail in check form from his regular bank account. Better still there could be a salary savings plan where on every date of receipt of funds of accountholder from his employer that a certain amount would be automatically sent from his recipient bank to this distant bank. Care would have to be taken to set the initial and subsequent recurring deposit from the master bank account to be of an amount, which would not interfere with the necessary monthly financial obligations of the accountholder. The amount set aside had to be the amount that would not affect or interfere with the normal course of the accountholder's life.

A few of the financial service professionals experimented with the distant bank approach and amassed substantial seed capital for their future financial activities including the opportunity to get involved in new business opportunities.

It is really important to realize that all future wealth creation starts with the first step in the mythical Chinese journey, referred to earlier. AND THAT CRITICAL FIRST STEP IN WEALTH CREATION IS SAVINGS. Saving money does not refer to a haphazard program of short-term spurts in savings followed by short-term spurts of spending.

Such financial activity would lead to very minimal results in capital creation and create a tremendous level of frustration for the investor. If such activity continues over a period of time it would also lead to a loss of financial self-confidence on part of the investor and cause distractions in achieving the goal of self-sufficiency and optimal wealth creation. For a savings program to be successful, it has to be a deliberate, consistent and ongoing process. There has to be an initial goal established. Depending on your financial self-discipline habits, past savings results and current lifestyle demands, you the investor, must set a goal, which is easily achievable. Say, you start with a goal of saving $10,000 in a 24-month period. You would need to save, on a consistent monthly basis around $400 per month to reach this goal. The first goal must be reached within the 24 month timeframe to build your confidence in your ability to save. If $400 per month appears to be achievable then stick to this goal. On the other hand, if you can only set aside, with some self-discipline, $300 per month, then proceed towards this goal. In the short term it does not matter whether you save $300 or $400 per month.

The investor should make a monthly budget enumerating all receipts of revenue, including employment and self-employment income and any other sources of income. The investor should also identify on paper all sources of expenses including living expenses, credit card bills, and etcetera. If one finds that there is very little net income left after expenses, one has to rethink and re-appraise one's financial priorities.

Tearing up all unnecessary credit cards and reducing debt would help free up some net income for your savings goal. THE KEY TO SAVINGS SUCCESS IS TO ACHIEVE YOUR INITIALLY ESTABLISHED SAVINGS GOAL. THIS GOAL MUST BE REACHED WITHIN THE TIME ALLOCATED FOR ITS COMPLETION. The new financial self-confidence achieved by using this method will lead to setting newer and higher savings goals in the future.

With respect to the above savings method outlined, the other general rule to be followed is that you cannot allow too much capital to accumulate at one time in any one place. Money, by its very nature, needs to be circulated in order to generate more wealth. Money, which is hoarded, results in a negative impact on future wealth creation.

Let us look at an example to elucidate this. Say, you set and achieve a financial goal of saving $20,000 in 24 months.

As soon as you reach this goal you must do two things:
1. Set and embark on a new financial savings goal.
2. Remove this $20,000 and invest it in a worthwhile investment cause like down payment on a new home, investment in a good mutual fund, down payment for establishing a new business, etcetera. While you are growing your capital as a direct result of smart savings strategies, you must be aware and abide by the following rule:

RULE. Accumulation of principal is more important than accumulation of interest on principal. If you have embarked on a program to save $20000 over 24 months, the focus must be on building principal first. You may, in the process of reaching your goal, get distracted by considering how you can grow the money saved so far at a faster pace by investing the savings proceeds in higher yield investments. Nothing could be more distracting or damaging with respect to achievement of this mid-term goal of savings. DO NOT ALLOW YOURSELF TO BE DISTRACTED OR LOSE FOCUS OF YOUR PRINCIPAL GOAL OF ACCUMULATING $20,000 FIRST. You have your whole life to grow this principal. You must apply all your mental, emotional and nervous energy in achieving the challenging task of gathering the PRINCIPAL SAVINGS OF $20,000 FIRST.

DO NOT TRY TO DO TOO MUCH, TOO QUICKLY OR YOU MAY FAIL IN YOUR INITIAL SAVINGS ENDEAVOR. REMEMBER, FIRST THINGS FIRST........................

To summarize this challenge of savings, we must accept the PRINCIPLE OF COMPROMISE AND SACRIFICE. The only way you can save money consistently and successfully over a short or mid-period of time is to forego some of the luxuries and desires you have today. There is no shortcut to effective savings. If you are living at close to 100 per cent of your current income, you must be willing to make some hard choices and sacrifices in order to save something today. Some of the effective ways of saving more money short and long-term are:

SOLUTION 1.

SPEND LESS THAN YOU EARN.

This was discussed earlier. However, saying this is easier than actually doing it. You must get the full co-operation and support of your spouse or other significant partner in this journey towards financial excellence and independence. You must work together with your family, if you have one, to explain to everyone why you are embarking on this journey, how the funds will come in handy to your family and specifically how long everyone will have to sacrifice some comforts and luxuries to meet with some of the family's long-term goals like educational funding for children, your retirement goals, emergency funds for periods of unemployment, disability or business bankruptcy. Greatest results will be reached if you bring your entire family on-board with your short, mid-term and long-term financial goals.

You must be able to sell them on the value of such short, mid and long-term financial sacrifice.

SOLUTION 2.

EARN MORE INCOME—SPEND AS YOU DO NOW.

This is more a mid or long-term challenge. To earn more income, you must seek ways within the framework of your life now to gain more education. You must also improve the quality and nature of your work experience in order to be of more value to either your current or new employer. You must accentuate your sales and negotiation skills to move you to a higher level of value in your job or business.

More income comes through your ability to become a more productive individual to your employer or business. This obviously would take some time, proper planning and accurate identification of the skills and experience required to enhance your income.

SOLUTION 3.
EARN MORE——SPEND LESS.

his represents the fastest way to build your savings goal. Savings represent the seed capital for future wealth creation.

THE AMERICAN SAVINGS QUANDARY.

The United States is one of the wealthiest nations in the world. In this country, many people take a lot of material things for granted. There is great thought given to choices of lifestyle.

A fairly decent apartment or house, a car, a color TV, one 14 day vacation a year, 2 paid days leave on weekends and three good quality meals constitute the minimum needs for most of the populace. From this point on, there is great emphasis on choice and exercise of a better lifestyle. In so many other parts of the world, what Americans consider a basic need is really a luxury and unachievable dream for many people. In spite of all the abundance of wealth and prosperity in their working lifetime, it is a known fact that the majority of Americans fail to plan for their retirement. Even fewer Americans achieve millionaire status.

Why is it, that in one of the richest nations on earth, the populace cannot achieve financial independence and a good savings record????? In fact, the U.S. boasts a negative savings rate currently. If the U.S. negative savings rate in the year 2002 is published as being -2%, this means in layman terms, that out of a gross income of $100 earned by an American, his expenses account for $102. This results in exposure to a debt of $2 per $100 earned. This deficiency of $2 per $100 is normally financed through loans provided generously (and often indiscriminately) by banks, credit card companies and other financial institutions.

Several Americans in this predicament make a false presumption that savings can only be made by them setting aside large amounts of money initially. Since they feel they do not possess the wherewithal to generate such large amounts of savings initially because of large monthly financial commitments they feel the whole savings exercise is futile.

This psychological visualization of scarcity for an average American creates a great obstacle to the orderly creation of a systematic savings program. So, an average working class individual gets beaten down mentally and emotionally before he can even take a single positive step towards saving capital. If one can even start saving $10 per month consistently one can gradually build a nest egg for the future. Wealth will inevitably follow financial sacrifice, self-discipline and commitment.

As soon as some wealth is developed, the level of investor confidence will increase. With this confidence will come the ability to visualize and execute the future saving of larger amounts of capital on a consistent basis. Motivation, therefore, plays a bigger role than most investors know or believe in, with respect to achievement of financial independence through savings. NEVER IGNORE THE POWERFUL IMPACT OF SAVINGS ON YOUR FUTURE FINANCIAL SUCCESS!!!!!!!!!!!!

CHAPTER 6

SECOND PILLAR OF YOUR FINANCIAL FOUNDATION - INVESTMENTS

LEARN TO INVEST - SIMPLE LESSONS IN INVESTING

The second pillar of your financial foundation is learning to understand and apply good investment techniques to grow your capital (acquired through consistent savings).An investment is defined as, "an opportunity to earn a return on your pool of capital." It goes without further explanation that the higher the return required by the investor, the greater the inherent risk in any investment made by such investor. Risk, in this context, is defined as

the chance taken by the investor of losing some or all of his principal investment, in pursuit of a gain in the marketplace. The broader definition of an investment is "the application of capital in a desired/needed area for intention of producing a desired result."

An important psychological principle why investors exert capital, time and energy to increase their wealth is the value such wealth has in making them feel more secure. Investors also believe they can fulfill one or more needs by becoming rich.

They believe that such need fulfillment forms the wellspring of their desire to increase their fortune and personal balance sheet.

MASLOW'S MODEL OF HUMAN NEEDS

ILLUSTRATION 2.

**MASLOW'S MODEL
HIERARCHY OF HUMAN NEEDS**

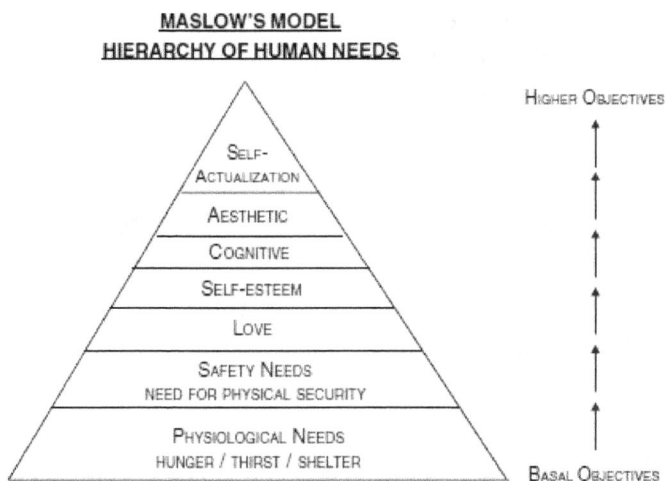

In the '50s a prominent psychologist, Abraham Maslow underlined a well developed hierarchy of human needs. Maslow's model of human needs is sometimes depicted in the form of a pyramid (see illustration 2). At the bottom of the pyramid are the basic needs. These are physiological needs like hunger, thirst and need for shelter. Once an individual fulfils these needs, he attempts to exert himself to move up the pyramid to achieve the next level of needs. These are normally safety needs. Safety needs represent the need to feel safe and secure and out of danger.

Once this level of need is fulfilled, a person tries to achieve the love and belonging need --- a need to be loved and experience a sense of affiliation and belonging to his reference group. There are four levels of needs above this in natural progression for fulfillment by an individual. In order of progression, they are self-esteem needs, which necessitate the need to gain approval and recognition from others. The next level encompasses cognitive needs, which represent the need to explore and understand things around oneself and one's environment. The next level is that of aesthetic needs which comprise of an understanding and appreciation of beauty both within and without in nature.

The final level of needs is the self-actualization need, which encompasses finding one's true self and understanding of one's ego and relationship with humanity and the world at large. This also involves being able to express oneself creatively and realize one's God given potential. If one sees the logic of a well organized hierarchy of human needs and the premise that we, as humans are constantly striving to meet multiple needs in logical order, then one can use the same thinking in constructing a human investment need suitability pyramid.

Illustration 3 on the next page expresses an investment pyramid, which is based on how investor's view the goals they need fulfilled through different investment schemes. The nature and composition of such goals is based on what particular need that investor believes is most valuable at a particular point of time. It shows how most investors understand and organize their personal needs with respect to investments and how this motivation for fulfillment of specific needs powers their approach towards engaging in various types of investments. One approach to such investment profiling is to accept investor's assuming a prioritized approach to investment of capital.

Illustration 3

**RAJPAL
INVESTMENT SUITABILITY PYRAMID©
BASED ON HIERARCHY OF INVESTOR NEEDS**

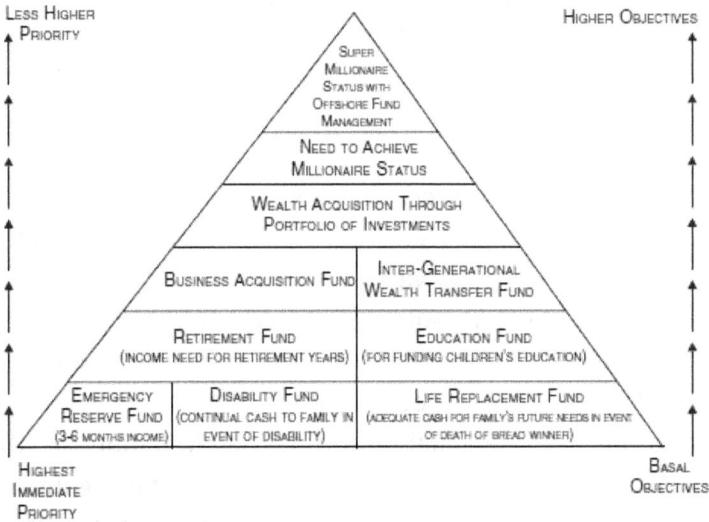

LESS HIGHER PRIORITY

HIGHER OBJECTIVES

SUPER MILLIONAIRE STATUS WITH OFFSHORE FUND MANAGEMENT

NEED TO ACHIEVE MILLIONAIRE STATUS

WEALTH ACQUISITION THROUGH PORTFOLIO OF INVESTMENTS

BUSINESS ACQUISITION FUND

INTER-GENERATIONAL WEALTH TRANSFER FUND

RETIREMENT FUND (INCOME NEED FOR RETIREMENT YEARS)

EDUCATION FUND (FOR FUNDING CHILDREN'S EDUCATION)

EMERGENCY RESERVE FUND (3-6 MONTHS INCOME)

DISABILITY FUND (CONTINUAL CASH TO FAMILY IN EVENT OF DISABILITY)

LIFE REPLACEMENT FUND (ADEQUATE CASH FOR FAMILY'S FUTURE NEEDS IN EVENT OF DEATH OF BREAD WINNER)

HIGHEST IMMEDIATE PRIORITY

BASAL OBJECTIVES

79

Since time, energy and capital are finite and fixed in nature, the investor must make a choice as to where an investment is made and how much risk he is prepared to undertake in the fulfillment of his return expectation He must also assign a priority to the need which must be fulfilled as a direct result of such investment. Based on the urgency of the need, from his unique individual perspective, the investor then decides whether or not to engage in a specific investment scheme.

From an ideal, unbiased perspective, priority must be defined as the need for cash by the investor in the event of a financial emergency. If one accepts such a premise as being valid, then it is understandable that one must follow this investment suitability pyramid depicted (in illustration 3) to understand how an investor must distribute his money to achieve the best financial outcome long-term. When we review the need of an investor in what appears to him to be a financial emergency, we must, importantly, understand how he views a financial emergency. A financial emergency could be any urgent, impending need for capital by the investor at a particular point of time. The need for capital at specific points of time may change based on the personal and financial situation of the investor and is influenced by varying complex environmental demands. There is no hard and fast rule as to what need will present a demand at a particular point of time.

An astute investor will project the varying demands which may be placed on his capital at different points of time in the future and construct an investment pyramid in his mind which would fulfill these demands at different points in his financial life. This is where this investment pyramid depicted, becomes handy as a mental and visualization tool for a practical investor in arranging and organizing his affairs to meet with any future need or cash emergency. If one looks at the graphical exposition of the investment pyramid one can note that the most obvious and desirable goal of achieving super-millionaire status is at the peak of the pyramid. There obviously exists a temptation to sidestep all the necessary bottom steps and get to the peak of super-millionaire status by taking some shortcuts. Unfortunately, there are no shortcuts. The road to wealth and prosperity appears to be a long one for most investors.

One can considerably reduce the time to achieve this millionaire status by understanding, accepting and implementing this investment pyramid on a step-by-step basis. This is not to say that we do not have instant or super-fast millionaires in this world. Every day, instant millionaires are being created by national lottery schemes. However, these millions are being dissipated as fast as they are won. We are seeking a long-term, permanent situation where not only does an investor accumulate or win capital but also can maintain, protect and enhance this value. If such is the goal of an investor, there is no short cut to financial success.

As it is with savings goals outlined in the earlier chapter, the financial foundation must be established first. This pyramid suggests that an investor attempt to secure and achieve basal objectives (objectives shown in the basal areas of pyramid above) first.

Once these financial needs have been fulfilled by setting aside adequate amounts of capital, then and only then can the peak area of millionaire status be achieved.

This investment pyramid can be likened to an experienced mountaineer trying to climb Mount Everest, the highest mountain peak in the world. To get to the peak of the mountain he must go through the travails and struggles of starting at the base and slowly climb his way up to success. Once the basal and mid level of the mountain are scaled, the mountaineer places himself in a position to scale the highest peak. FIRST THINGS FIRST.

Let us now review the investment pyramid in detail. The basal objectives right at the bottom of the pyramid have been shown as the highest priority areas. The reason for labeling them as the highest priority areas is that these needs, if not fulfilled, tend to pose the greatest danger to achievement of super-millionaire status. Some of these needs or basal most objectives are:

1. Establishment of a reserve emergency fund equivalent to three to six months of annual family income. This fund is to be utilized by the family in event of unexpected unemployment of any family member, amongst other things.

2. Continual cash to family in event of disability of any income earner in the family.

3. Continual cash to family to meet with their daily financial needs in event of death of either principal or secondary income earner.

To illustrate why these three needs are labeled as being of the highest priority, an illustration of the disability need is now elucidated. Let us assume that an investor's net worth today is $750,000. Let us further assume that his cash position today is $500,000. His cash position is the amount of cash he has access to, within a very short period of time, to be drawn on to meet any impending need. This investor now experiences a serious long-term illness and is forced off work for an undetermined period of time. Since he is not working and earning any income he is forced to draw on his hard earned capital to defray day-to-day expenses. His minimum monthly requirement to meet all personal and household expenses amounts to $3000 per month. Ignoring the inflation and interest value on investor capital, this investor would go through his $500,000 in less than 14 years. What is the value and significance of spending the time and energy to accumulate $500,000 and then turning around and seeing it go up in smoke in less than 14 years???? The intelligent investment plan would be for the investor to purchase an inexpensive disability insurance policy for $3000 per month. This policy would provide a regular income stream worth $3000 per month in the event of disability. The disability insurance company would take on the responsibility of funding the investor's needs of $3000 per month, thereby releasing any pressure on the investor's capital for cash flow.

If an investor purchased such a disability insurance policy to protect him and his family, he could turn around and invest the $500,000 cash in his portfolio.

At the end of fourteen years, assuming a 10% net average yearly return, his overall investment position would be worth 1.90 million dollars. What would you prefer achieving at the end of 14 years if you were faced with a long-term debilitating disease, which prevented you from working and earning any income? Would you prefer being bankrupt in 14 years or would you like to be the proud owner of 1.9 million dollars, then???? Such concerns bring forth the need for building a strong financial foundation first and protecting your long-term chances of not only building capital but also being able to hold on to capital in the event of unanticipated emergencies.

Another basal objective of extremely high priority is planning to have adequate cash to meet with your family's future needs in the event of death. Planning for one's death is one of the last things a person contemplates on. After all, we all sub-consciously believe that we are going to live forever. We are so engrossed in enjoying our lives and facing our numerous challenges that we fail to stop and see that one day the plug is going to be pulled and we are not going to be around. However, the reality is that we all must die sometime. Most of us leave a family or other loved ones behind when we die. And these loved ones count on us. Is it fair to say that some forward planning for their financial future is worthwhile? This is all life insurance is about. Forget the hype of life insurance. Forget about all the slick insurance salespeople you happen to meet. Forget all the scaremongers. All that life insurance ought to do is provide capital and a running stream of income for your loved ones when they need it the most——particularly when you are gone. Life insurance is not a luxury or pipedream. It is an absolute necessity. Therefore proper life insurance planning is considered a basal need of the highest priority.

Going upwards in the investment pyramid are two other needs of mid or long-term priority. Effective retirement planning early on in life and planning and executing a good educational funding plan for your children are very important priorities. Providing a separate fund to finance your children's education is crucial.

In most cases, unless you are super-rich, you must set aside money early on in your child's life and consistently keep accumulating adequate deposits to reach your educational funding goals. Education acquisition is a competitive factor influencing the future career of your children. The whole world has become extremely specialized. And children's future income and wealth are contingent on the acquisition of a set of skills in demand in the marketplace. Do you want your children to attain mediocrity or do you want them to have every opportunity to excel in their chosen careers and life path? The cost of education in quality universities is progressively climbing. If one is to add the ravaging costs of inflation to this cost of education, one is faced with a monstrous capital requirement for funding a college and university education.

As we progress upward on the investment pyramid scale we look at earmarking funds for starting or buying a business.

Also, as your wealth level increases, assuring transfer of your total wealth or estate to your loved ones (inter-generational wealth transfer) with the least amount of government of government taxes and red tape becomes crucial.

As we progress through your final stages of financial super-status we must deal with the next three progressive stages:

1. Growing wealth by creating and managing successfully an efficient portfolio with proper asset allocation and risk control strategies.

2. Final achievement of millionaire status.

3. Diversification of wealth into foreign offshore jurisdictions for a more permanent and secure financial footing.

It is important to note that some investors may not want to achieve millionaire status at home first before diversifying overseas. A host of factors may justify this move. Impending urgent business battles, impending bankruptcy, unreasonable claims by creditors, customers or a dissatisfied and estranged spouse may lead one to diversify overseas earlier to save some or all of one's hard earned wealth. Care should be taken by such investors not to break the law of their home country while executing such strategies. Going offshore, though, represents the only real and permanent security for most investors.

Away from the prying eyes of predators, in a safe and exclusive jurisdiction, an investor can breathe a sigh of relief --- knowing he has wealth to fall back on if times get tough at home. If properly structured and cared for, offshore investment vehicles perform the most important step in financial planning --- providing a permanent and private avenue for your hard-earned wealth.

CHAPTER 7

THIRD PILLAR OF YOUR FINANCIAL FOUNDATION – RISK MANAGEMENT

LEARN TO PROTECT

It is a national tragedy, that people, in general, do not understand the nature and functioning of insurance. A lot of the blame must rest on a combination of overzealous salesmen and a particular number of dishonest insurance companies, who love to misrepresent their products and/or sell unsuitable products to an unwitting public.

Insurance is very simply a risk management tool. There is a financial risk creating a need for cash in unforeseen emergencies. Such emergencies cannot be timed or forecast with any deal of certainty for a specific person. However, one thing is certain. Once this emergency unfolds unexpectedly, cash is required urgently to solve this financial problem. The role of insurance is to merely provide a fund of money to solve a financial problem, if and when, it occurs. If an investor had millions of spare dollars, he could possibly become his own insurer (insurance company). His millions of dollars would then act as a reserve providing cash to solve a financial problem arising out of sudden and unexpected disability, death or premature retirement. However, most of us do not fall into this category of super-millionaires.

We desperately and urgently need cash to solve impending financial crises, as and when such occur. Consider, for a moment, an insurance company as a provider of capital. They have an almost unlimited amount of capital available. This capital can be drawn down and used by an individual investor. Based on the type of arrangement or contract you establish with such insurance company, you, the investor can, on occurrence of a named contingency, receive specific amounts of cash flow for a specific time duration. The investor pays the insurance company a premium, which represents his cost for shifting any cash flow risk to the insurance company, which provides capital and cash flow to fund requirements in the event of specific emergencies, like death or disability (among other contingencies) .

In illustration 4A and 4B, one can understand the true nature of the relationship between an insured investor and an insurance company.

Illustration 4 A

INVESTOR - INSURANCE COMPANY RELATIONSHIP

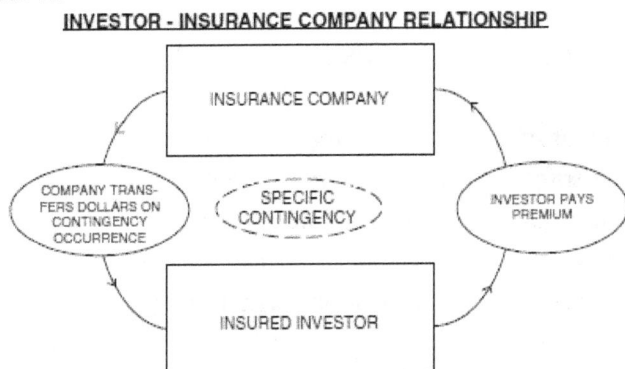

Illustration 4 B

LIST OF INVESTOR CONTINGENCIES

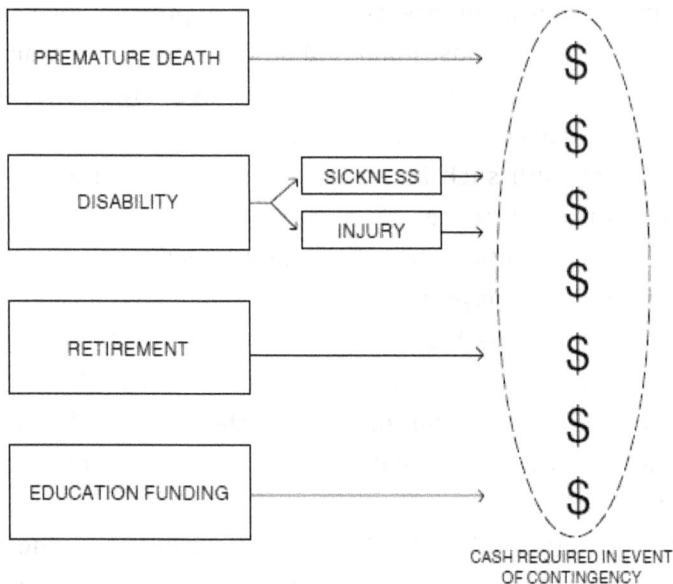

CASH REQUIRED IN EVENT
OF CONTINGENCY

INVESTOR – INSURANCE COMPANY RELATIONSHIP

LEARN TO PROTECT YOUR LOVED ONES

Life insurance is the primary risk management mechanism, which transfers dollars to your family in the event of your premature death. Several significant events occur when you die. On the one hand, your family is faced with the challenge of having enough cash flow to meet with their daily needs.

On the other hand, your family is probably faced with a significant or total loss of income when you, as a primary breadwinner disappear from the face of this earth. Additionally, your family is faced with some immediate cash demands. Uncle Sam is first in line. The Government wants all unpaid taxes (from the deceased breadwinner's estate) first. The family also faces the task of paying off several creditors, like credit card companies who normally require all outstanding balances paid off immediately.

Then there are cash requirements for funeral expenses. Most families face a double whammy effect --- one the emotional loss of a loved one and secondly a financial loss as creditors knock on their door.

Under such circumstances, life insurance becomes the only feasible provider of capital.

CASH REQUIRED IN EVENT OF CONTINGENCY

Some of the money required by a family (in the event of death of the primary breadwinner) is categorized below. Money is required on an urgent basis to pay for:

1. Funeral expenses of the deceased.

2. For the establishment of an emergency fund for financial re-adjustment of the family. The emergency fund also serves as a short-term cash cushion to meet with any unanticipated cash requirements.

3. For the establishment and funding of education for children.

4. For possibly paying off the mortgage on the deceased's principal residence, thereby enabling the family to live in the same neighborhood without the burden of making monthly mortgage payments.

5. For the establishment of an income fund. This income fund would serve as a method of replacing a percentage of the deceased's income and ensure a stable and consistent source of income to the family thereby providing financial stability in a time of crises.

6. For the establishment of a retirement fund to the surviving spouse, thereby guaranteeing her financial freedom and independence after the death of a loved one.

The major role of insurance is to provide capital and income to the investor's family on terms and conditions suitable to such investor. A life insurance policy represents a contract between two parties --- the insurance company being the party of the first part and the investor or insured being the party of the second part. The insurance contract or policy specifies the amount of capital to be paid out to the insured/insured's family in the event of specific contingencies like death, disability or retirement. In exchange for this privilege afforded, the insured pays a premium at certain frequencies to the insurance company.

Illustration 4 C

LIST OF CONTINGENCIES (continued)

Money transfer to estate / beneficiary
of insured on
occurrence of contingency

LIFE INSURANCE	CONTINGENCY 1. Natural Death 2. Accidental Death	INSURED INVESTOR

Pays Premium

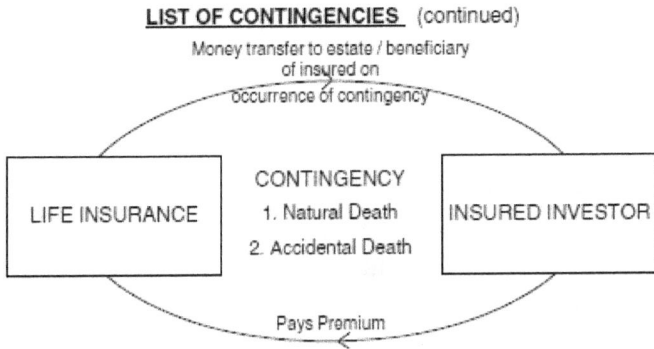

Illustration 4C explains this transfer of capital concept. In short, the premium is the price the investor pays to allow an insurance company to assume the risk of providing capital/cash flow to either himself or his loved ones.

The amount of premium you pay is based on whether, in addition to protection you require to:

1. Stabilize your premium level during the entire contract period with the insurance company AND

2. If there is any investor expectation in building up some cash/investment values in the insurance policy.

LEARN TO PROTECT YOUR BUSINESS

For a significant portion of the American public, the entrepreneurial spirit is very much alive. For over 10% of the adult American population, a business represents a major source of income and livelihood. It follows, therefore, that protection of the Family unincorporated business or Family Corporation is important.

What is additionally important is protection of any income and profits from such family business/corporation in the event of death or disability of the business owner or shareholder. Simple insurance structures exist to protect business partner's families in the event of death or disability of such businessmen. One such insurance structure is an insurance policy within which such business partners are protected. Each business partner places an investment value on his business interest in such partnership while alive.

This investment value represents the net market value of the business partner's interest in a specific business. In the event of such partner's death, the insurance company pays the deceased business partner's family his total investment in the business. Say, a business

has two partners. Each partner pays the premium for a life insurance policy on the other partner. The face amount or value of each policy corresponds with the net market value of the business partner's interest. In the event of one partner's death, the surviving partner can own the business outright. The cost of a nominal insurance premium assures the surviving business partner ownership of the entire business.

The deceased partner's family is also satisfied that they have received the full-undiluted market value of the business partner's share. A buy-sell agreement seals this exchange. Very simply, what the buy-sell agreement does is to set a price on each partner's business interest at a specific point of time. The agreement specifies that when one business partner dies, his family/legal heirs must sell his partnership share to the surviving partner/ partners. In exchange for this promise, the deceased partner's family must necessarily receive a lump sum death benefit from the insurance company. This death benefit is equal to the value of the partner's business interest in the partnership. In this way, the surviving partner is happy that he does not have to welcome a new, unknown stranger to the business. The entire partnership business is his exclusively. The deceased partner's family is also happy that they have realized fair value for their investment in the business.

Do note that the surviving partner has paid the insurance company a premium for this privilege and thereby guaranteed 100% ownership and control of the business. What a small price to pay to own a business. Everyone walks away happy from the table.

This business arrangement is visually expressed in illustration 5.

Illustration 5

SAMPLE BUY - SELL
PARTNERSHIP AGREEMENT FUNDED BY LIFE INSURANCE

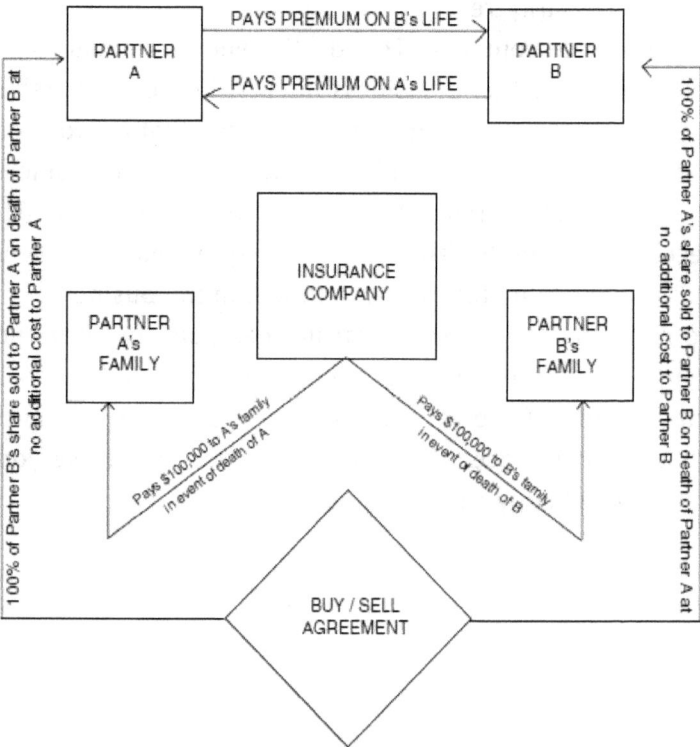

LEARN TO PROTECT YOUR RETIREMENT INCOME NEEDS

Retirement marks an important turning point in one's life. Unfortunately, most people do not plan adequately for their golden years of retirement. They don't plan because retirement seems to be too far away. Most people are more concerned with "putting water on today's fires"--- dealing with the ceaseless never ending pressure of paying today's bills like mortgage payments, tax and social security obligations and spending the necessary money to raise a family.

It is a tragedy that most working families cannot distinguish the "forest from the trees." They are so engrossed with today's problems and financial pressures that they simply cannot shut their eyes and take some "time out" to review their long-term needs for retirement.

Retirement is guaranteed to arrive for most of us as much as are the twin certainties of death and taxes. We all must retire at some point in our working life --- the only variables are at what age and with how much income. Do not forget that the only real thing we can count on is income flowing in from our investments (made during our lifetime). Government sponsored retirement schemes may or may not be around when we are ready to retire. In an ever-changing world nothing is guaranteed --- not our jobs nor our businesses.

Therefore, the earlier you start socking money away for your retirement needs, the better your quality of life will be when you are too old or too weak to work.

With respect to designing an effective retirement investment strategy, one must first use all available tax shelters available for retirement planning. The logic behind this is simple. If you get a tax break by investing in a qualified retirement investment vehicle like an IRA (Individual retirement account in the U.S.), then you have a more cost effective way of building retirement values in such a plan as compared to investing in a non-tax deferred retirement investment plan.

Employer sponsored retirement schemes are also an effective way of saving towards retirement.

LEARN TO PROTECT YOUR CHILDREN'S EDUCATION NEEDS

In my dealings with clients, I find most people take extreme positions on planning and executing an education strategy for their children. Some overzealously plan for their children's educational future. Others are simply paralyzed and do absolutely nothing. A more preferable approach would be the adoption of a common ground. Such a common ground would adopt a more balanced approach, taking into account not only your children's future needs but also your other priorities like retirement needs, emergency fund needs, etcetera (in line with the investment pyramid propounded on earlier).

First and foremost, one must understand and accept that undergraduate and postgraduate education constitute critical elements for your child's future economic success. Identifying your child's aptitude, skills and talents form the first step in building a good educational foundation.

Solid psychological testing with the objective of isolating critical competitive strengths (of your children) is important. Once this evaluation is complete, optional successful careers for your child must be studied. All roads involving long-term educational success for your child lead to enrolment in a good university. There is no question that an Ivy League School represents the best educational investment for your child.

A Master's degree in a high demand occupational field from an Ivy League School would provide the best probability of entry into a Fortune 500 company at a high initial salary. After that, a lot depends on your child's contribution to the business enterprise he serves.

With respect to protecting your children's education needs, two parallel situations must be simultaneously considered and planned for. Some investors set aside separately monies whose ultimate purpose is to fund their children's education. This is the first important planning tool.

However, the next parallel-planning situation is critical. This situation automatically funds the entire gross amount required for the children's education in the event of premature death of the investor. For example, let us assume you are planning to set aside $100,000 for your son's education.

The first parallel-planning situation would calculate a periodic payment or a lump sum payment, which would after application of a conservative interest amount yield $100,000 (at the end of a stipulated period of time).

The second parallel-planning situation would earmark an insurance policy (on the life of the investor) with face value of $100,000. This would create an immediate estate of $100,000 which would finance your son's education if you did not live long enough to accumulate that required amount of capital.

Both parallel-planning investment strategies are crucial to the long-term success of your plans to generate the necessary funds for your children's education.

LEARN TO PROTECT YOUR WEALTH IN EVENT OF DISABILITY

Disability can be viewed as any physical or mental condition, which prevents you from working and engaging in your current avocation.

Several forms of disability exist. You might experience a situation where your health is so bad that you are FULLY DISABLED. On the other hand you might become (as a result of a car accident) physically impaired, a condition which may not allow you to work a regular 40-hour week but may offer you the ability to work for a limited period of time, say, 20 hours per week. This condition is defined as one of PARTIAL DISABILITY.

Care must be taken to protect your hard-earned wealth from financial loss resulting from a loss of income due to either total or partial disability. A physical condition preventing you from work could be an injury arising as a result of a job related accident. More serious conditions like a serious heart attack or cancer could create a long-term forced absence from work. Stress is a very common example of a psychological condition, which could impair your ability to work.

During periods of disability one becomes painfully aware of the sharp reduction of income --- or in the most extreme conditions of total disability the complete loss of income. One is usually used to a certain routine of work and one mistakenly assumes that the income derived from such work will always be available. A disability represents a rude wake-up call for most investors.

Life and its attendant financial responsibilities continue even in the event of a disability --- however, income is drastically reduced or completely absent during such periods of sickness or injury.

The sad and tragic part of a disability is the fact that life must still go on if you are sick or injured. The bills must still get paid in the presence of less income --- this is a perfect recipe for bankruptcy and marital strife. The majority of the working populace, unfortunately, do not take disability planning very seriously.

Let me illustrate the danger of losing your hard-earned wealth pretty quickly. Meet John who is an independent businessman. His net income for the calendar year 2001 was $100,000.

John is married and has two kids. His business has been established for five years. John has a group insurance policy at his place of work. To save costs, he has only purchased a short-term group disability policy which replaces/pays two-thirds of his net income for 91 days. John works long hours in his business and is fairly good at what he does. One day, John suffers a stroke. He is hospitalized for a week. He is subsequently discharged from the hospital and advised to take rest at home under strict nursing supervision for several months. John's group insurance policy will provide him with two-thirds of his income, i.e. $ 100,000 x 66.66% divided by 12 = $ 5555/month approximately. The insurance company pays him $ 5555 per month for a period of ninety-one days. After that, John is completely on his own. What is John going to do for money after three months????

These are some of the bills John needs to keep paying on a continual basis after three months:

RESIDENCE COSTS
House mortgage payment
Car insurance premium
Life insurance premium
House insurance premium
Grocery costs
Education costs for children
Credit card bills
Car payments
Phone and cable TV costs
Electricity and water bills

BUSINESS COSTS

Payroll costs

Office rent and related costs.

Replacement cost of hiring an executive on a part-time basis to do his function as chief executive of his company.

WHERE WILL JOHN FIND THE MONEY TO MAKE THESE PAYMENTS???????

There are only two ways of generating cash --- the first is by way of an individual working and the second is having your money work for you. Since John is not working but still has personal (residence) costs and corporate (business) costs, his only choice is to use his hard-earned personal cash and business savings to fund his obligations. How long could John survive without earning a regular income from his business???

The moral of this story is really in the form of a question to you, the serious, hard-working investor:

How long could you and your family survive without earning any income from your job or business?

A corollary to this question is:

Have you calculated how many months you could survive if you are forced off work due to a serious accident or illness?

These questions are not intended to scare you. The questions are only designed to ask you if you have done efficient forward disability planning to protect your hard-earned wealth.

According to U.S. Government Disability Insurance Statistics, you have a greater chance of experiencing a loss due to disability than of experiencing a loss due to either your house burning down or due to a car accident. You, however, buy car and house insurance without hesitation. But purchase of disability insurance causes nervousness and indecision. Why do you hesitate in insuring your most valuable asset? This asset is your earning power. It represents your ability to get up in the morning healthy with an attendant capacity to use your talents and experience in work generating a constant flow of income. The ignorance and confusion surrounding disability insurance is unfathomable.

To summarize this third pillar of your financial foundation --- risk management is critical to your long-term success. The concepts surrounding effective risk management are very simple. You know that there may be certain calamities in your life.

If and when such calamities arise, you will require cash at real short notice. When such a requirement of cash comes to the fore you have one of two choices:

1. Either to pay the necessary money (to honor your responsibilities) by using your hard-earned wealth or

2. Using someone else's money.

A good businessman will try to shift the risk of providing capital for his needs to a third party like an insurance company. By paying a nominal premium ranging from 1% to 5% of the risk covered one can effectively shift the financial burden of providing cash to another entity.

By doing this you effectively protect 95 to 99% of your investor fortune/capital, which would otherwise (in the absence of insurance) be gobbled up in the event of death or disability. This allows your nest egg (sans the small disability insurance premium) to grow without interruption and guarantees a larger pool of capital for your future super-millionaire status.

CHAPTER 7

FOURTH PILLAR OF YOUR FINANCIAL FOUNDATION
— EFFECTIVE TAX MANAGEMENT OF YOUR RESOURCES

Taxes represent an onerous burden on wealth creation and accumulation. Taxes represent a demand by a sovereign government on money earned by its citizens and foreign workers. The concept of jurisdiction here is particularly important. Generally, your state of residence and its affiliation nationally determine your tax level. If you live in San Francisco, California and earn most of your income there you are considered a California and U.S. tax resident. Your federal tax rate is set by your Adjusted Gross Income (AGI). The U.S. is however one of the harshest countries in the world as far as taxation is concerned. The U.S. Government taxes a citizen's worldwide income irrespective of residence. That means, that if you are an American and live and work in Canada for nine months in a year and reside in the U.S. for the remaining three months, you must still file a U.S. tax return for your income in Canada along with your income earned in the U.S. Most of the advanced countries in the world only charge their citizens tax if they reside in that specific country. Your taxes are comprised of both direct visible taxes and indirect hidden taxes.

DIRECT VISIBLE TAXES
1. FEDERAL INCOME TAX
2. STATE INCOME TAX
3. CITY AND COUNTY TAX.

INDIRECT AND SOMETIMES HIDDEN TAXES
1. SALES TAX ON GOODS PURCHASED.
2. LIQUOR /GASOLINE TAX. (HIDDEN IN PRICE OF PRODUCT)

OTHER TAXES

1. GIFT TAX——LEVIED ON GIFTS GIVEN OVER A CERTAIN AMOUNT EVERY YEAR.
2. ESTATE TAX—LEVIED ON GROSS PROCEEDS OF ESTATE OVER A CERTAIN AMOUNT WHEN INDIVIDUAL DIES.
3. TAXES ON DIVIDENDS EARNED ON SHARES OF PUBLICLY TRADED COMPANIES.
4. SHORT TERM CAPITAL GAIN TAX.
5. LONG TERM CAPITAL GAIN TAX.
6. TAXES ON INTEREST INCOME FROM BANK DEPOSITS, PREFERRED SHARES, BOND INTEREST.

With all the taxes charged by Uncle Sam --- it is not a wonder that most taxpayers seek ways of deferring or avoiding taxes.

Organizing your affairs to pay the least amount of tax is very legal. However, willfully avoiding the declaration of your income is a very serious offence and can land you in jail with a stiff penalty and/or a jail term.

From an investment perspective, paying taxes slows down the growth of your hard-earned nest egg. Let's say you had a nest egg of $250,000.You want to build this up rather quickly. After sitting with your tax advisor and determining the tax ramifications of your future investment of $250,000, you figure out the following:

1. Investment of a sum of $250,000 is to be executed.

2. Your anticipated return is projected at 14 per cent per annum.

3. Your projected marginal tax rate is 30 per cent—you project a loss of around 4 per cent per year in taxes to the Government as a result of having to pay taxes on capital gains generated by your investment. This capital gain is assumed to attract an annual tax liability of approximately 4% every year.

Now, let us see what would happen if you were able to organize your affairs in such a way that you paid no taxes on this investment versus paying 4 per cent taxes annually as projected earlier. As you can see above, a one-time $250,000 investment was projected to generate

$ 3,435,000 in return after 20 years if no taxes were paid during accumulation versus the same investment generating $ 1,682,500 if taxes were paid. What a difference a four percent tax level

Illustration 6

TAX - FREE v TAXABLE INVESTMENT

TAX - FREE INVESTMENT		TAXABLE INVESTMENT	
Initial Investment	$250,000	Initial Investment	$250,000
Average Annual Growth Rate	14% per year	Average Annual Growth Rate	14% per year
Tax	-0% per year	Less Annual Tax	-4% per year
Net Growth Rate	14%	Net Growth Rate	10%
Return after 20 years	$3,435,000	Return after 20 years	$1,682,500
RETURN DIFFERENCE	$1,752,500		

TAX – FREE v TAXABLE INVESTMENT

RETURN DIFFERENCE $1,752,500 made in 20 years!!!!! The no-tax investment scenario generated approximately 1.75 million dollars more for the investor. Such a difference of $ 1.75 million is astronomical. This is the price you pay for being a tax-resident of the U.S.

This kind of thinking caused many Americans to move their money offshore where there was an absence of direct or indirect taxes and where 100 percent of your capital could grow freely without any hindrance or encumbrance. In addition, there was a possibility, that if the nest egg was structured efficiently, it could be 100 percent judgment proof from both U.S. and international court creditors.

SIMPLIFIED ASSET PROTECTION CONCEPTS

Asset protection represents one of the principal reasons for going offshore. Offshore is defined in this context as moving your assets physically from your country of residence to a foreign country to escape the undesirable pressures forced on your wealth. Such pressures include but are not limited to the following areas:

1. Frivolous lawsuits.
2. Liability lawsuits particularly for professionals like doctors, lawyers, accountants and sports athletes.
3. Liability claims in car accidents involving third party injury.
4. Kidnapping ransom demands.
5. Aggressive legal claims from an estranged spouse.
6. Creditor claims.
7. Unreasonable and unfair tax claims from the Internal Revenue Service.

Over the last decade, billions of dollars from advanced economies have found their way to exotic offshore locations.

These countries offer a more favorable home for your hard earned wealth with zero or minimal taxes on your capital growth.

One of the major advantages of moving assets offshore is the fact that you can effectively protect such assets by transferring it to a new jurisdiction (away from your home). The U.S. courts have zero or very limited control if your assets are lodged in a foreign country.

Even if a creditor was successful in locating your assets in such foreign jurisdiction --- he would have to chase you legally in a court of that jurisdiction to recover your money. This takes time, effort and legal costs on part of creditor involved. Therefore, movement of assets away from your country offers the first level of protection. However, in most cases, a strategy of this nature is not sufficient to provide you with maximum asset protection. Titling assets in the name of an International Business Company or even better in the name of a Trust offers more improved asset protection advantages.

CHAPTER 8

FIFTH PILLAR OF YOUR FINANCIAL FOUNDATION ---ESTATE PLANNING

THE NEED FOR EFFECTIVE INTER-GENERATIONAL WEALTH TRANSFER

Estate taxes levied represent a major loss of wealth for investors. An estate is merely a "corpus" where all assets are funneled into after the death of an investor. In the U.S. even life insurance proceeds are counted as part of an estate. To make matters worse, the estate tax liability must be paid to the Government in a relatively short period of time --- failing which the Government can seize your assets and sell them in an auction to generate cash to pay the tax liability. A lot of investors may be wealthy on paper with assets distributed in businesses, stocks, bonds and real estate. However, their estate may not have adequate liquid cash to pay the government their fair share of estate tax. This unfavorable liquidity could create a state of forced liquidation of investor assets by the Government in their urge to recover estate tax. Such adverse Government action could also cause great pain to the beneficiaries when they see their father or mother's wealth go up in smoke almost overnight.

Several multi-million dollar estates have been seized by the U.S. government and sold at bargain basement prices to satisfy the tax debt, leaving virtually no monies to the rightful beneficiaries. Thus, estate planning for effective inter-generational wealth transfer is crucial to protect the value of hard-earned assets.

ONSHORE STRUCTURES --- LIFE INSURANCE AS CHEAP CREATOR OF WEALTH FOR ESTATE PLANNING

Life insurance constitutes the cheapest and most effective solution to creating cash in the event of premature death. This cash can then be used to pay the Government estate tax bill almost immediately. This effectively creates protection from forced liquidation of any assets in an estate. This also allows the beneficiaries to continue enjoying the benefits of any assets left to them.

For example, let us suppose your father (investor) leaves behind a multi-million dollar estate to you, his only son. The estate tax liability on this estate amounts to $2 million. Would it not be better if your father had purchased a 2 million dollar life insurance policy on his life years back as compared to you, his son searching to extract $ 2 million dollars cash at short notice from his (departing father's) estate??? On your father's premature death, the cash could be available to pay Uncle Sam immediately. You could then enjoy all the assets provided by your father and not be forced to liquidate a business or home in a fire-loss sale. And the cost of such a structure could be pennies on the dollar.

113

OFFSHORE STRUCTURES

Several offshore structures like international business companies, trusts and foundations can be set up. Such structures create a source of wealth outside your jurisdiction. Such structures might also be able to create an estate outside your home country not subject to estate taxes. This is, however, a very complex area. Care should be taken to structure your business affairs in a legal way to avoid penalties and fines in your country of residence.

CHAPTER 9

SIXTH PILLAR OF YOUR FINANCIAL FOUNDATION –
ACTIVE COST-CUTTING STRATEGIES

Illustration 7A

NET SURPLUS INCOME COUNTS !!!

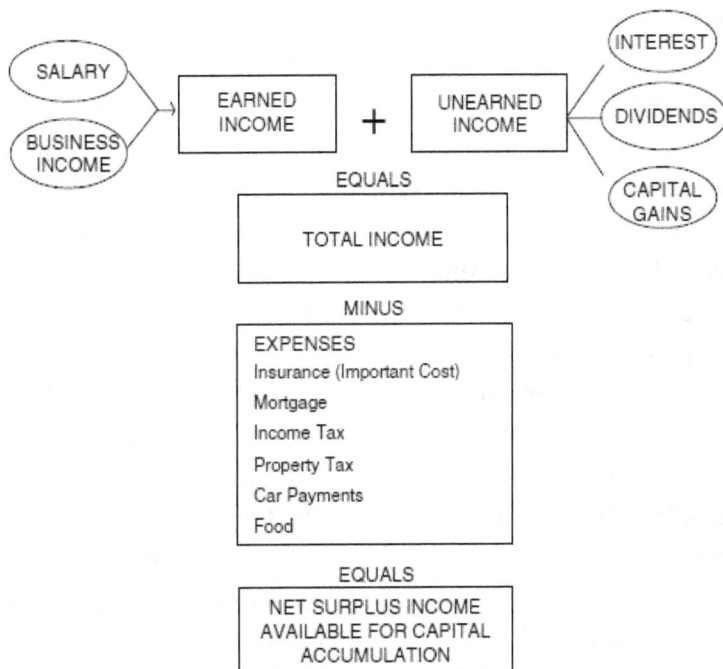

SALARY

BUSINESS INCOME

EARNED INCOME

+

UNEARNED INCOME

INTEREST

DIVIDENDS

CAPITAL GAINS

EQUALS

TOTAL INCOME

MINUS

EXPENSES
Insurance (Important Cost)
Mortgage
Income Tax
Property Tax
Car Payments
Food

EQUALS

NET SURPLUS INCOME
AVAILABLE FOR CAPITAL
ACCUMULATION

Cost control is an active exercise. To do this effectively you must be cognizant of all your sources of expense. You must realize and accept that the more living and day-to-day costs you cut, the more you have left over for savings and investments.

115

This pool of extra savings created in a systematic disciplined manner can accumulate a lot of wealth for an average investor over the long-term.

LEARN TO CUT COSTS OF ALL KINDS OF INSURANCE STRUCTURES

We will now deal with a significant drain on your future wealth --- the costs associated with insurance premiums for different types of required coverage's. In a broad sense, "What is insurance?" Insurance is probably best explained as a valuable risk management tool. Its only use is to control risk. For an investor, there is a risk of a future loss. The actual probability of loss of life, say, is difficult to visualize in an individual context (Although this risk is easily quantifiable mathematically).

For example, can you visualize yourself in a car accident this year? It is pretty hard to see your way ahead clear and give yourself a definite "Yes" or "No" answer to this question, isn't it? However, you do know that if you did have a car accident this year and injured someone else in this process that there exists some risk of a lawsuit from the injured party. This is where insurance comes in handy. You pay an insurance company a premium in exchange for which the insurance company guarantees to pay out a certain amount of money in the event of a specific contingency, e.g. covering your legal costs if an individual who gets injured in a car accident sues you. However, there is no end on how much you can spend on insurance premiums. Insurance companies realizing the presence of a myriad of contingencies, against which an investor might consider protection, have devised advanced marketing and advertising programs.

This, along with sophisticated well trained salespeople have resulted in unwitting investors either buying the wrong product or spending far more than is required to obtain protection against a contingency. Every salesperson has his "speal". The life insurance salesperson has his "speal." The car insurance salesperson has his "speal." The house insurance salesperson has his "speal." The insurance industry lands up paying higher commissions for higher premiums collected by their salespeople. Therefore any advice you receive from a salesperson is always biased and skewed towards collecting higher premiums than necessary. There is an in-built motivation for the salesperson to gather more premiums than what may be ordinarily required to insure against a contingency and most unfortunately, it is the individual insured investor who suffers monetarily. This investor becomes the solution to this never-ending demand from insurance companies to increase their premium and consequent profits. You, as an educated investor must realize this is happening in the marketplace and guard your premium costs as effectively and efficiently as possible, thereby increasing your wealth by keeping as much as you can with yourself. By reducing costs as much as possible while retaining important coverage's (to guard against future contingencies) you, the investor, are walking along the right financial path. In the area of necessary insurance coverage's, how does one separate truth from "crap"?

First, let us look at the most important contingencies, which need to be attended to in order of priority for most people:

1. LIFE INSURANCE. By far the most important need to be covered. However, an investor must view this as merely a mechanism to provide income to his family and meet with other cash demands in the event of his untimely death.

2. DISABILITY INSURANCE. This fills a critical need of providing dollars to keep you and your family afloat financially in the event that a disability prevents you from working and earning income. In some situations this may be equally or more important than life insurance.

3. MEDICAL INSURANCE. To provide full or supplemental coverage to reimburse you for consultation with physicians, surgeons, pay for hospital bills and drug expenses. If, you, as an investor do not have group medical insurance benefits, then this area of coverage could have a very high level of priority (at the same level) as life and disability insurance.

4. HOME INSURANCE. : To protect your home and contents in event of loss due to fire, theft and vandalism.

5. AUTOMOBILE INSURANCE: To protect you from third party claims for damage to other people and their property. Secondarily, to provide funds to repair your car in the event of a car accident and to provide for medical re-imbursement of your expenses, resulting from injury in a car accident.

6. BUSINESS INSURANCE: To protect your business from losses arising out of fire, vandalism and theft.

7. PARTNERSHIP INSURANCE. : A special form of insurance, which would give an individual an opportunity to buy out, his partner's equity interest in a shared business concern in the event of the other partner's death or disability.

8. PROFESSIONAL LIABILITY INSURANCE: A special form of coverage, which would provide funds to pay for your legal bills and any court judgment against you in any action, brought against you by your customers alleging negligence, misrepresentation or fraud. This may be an extremely high priority area for some professionals like physicians, surgeons, dentists or financial service professionals who are constantly dispensing advice.

AND THE INSURANCE LIST GOES ON AND ON...............

There is an American saying that goes like this, You can be insurance poor". In layman's terms this means that you could be paying so much in insurance premiums that you have no money left to live on (you are poor or insurance poor). Looking at the issue of insurance costs more deeply, how much must one spend as a percentage of gross income on insurance? There is no hard and fast figure—however I would like to suggest that it should not exceed a total of 15 to 20 percent of your gross income. In fact, if you can reduce it downwards more without compromising the necessary coverage's you require, then more power to you. However, the priority areas and worthwhile product considerations are as follows:

LIFE INSURANCE
Most preferable product—Universal Life.
Second best product—Level term insurance to age 65.

Least favorable product—Five year renewable and convertible term insurance to age 65. I would only recommend you use this product if you are on a tight financial budget and require a lot of life insurance coverage and are willing to convert it into a universal life policy in the near future.

DISABILITY INSURANCE

Best policy is one, which covers at least 60-65 percent of your current income for at least five years with a lifetime injury benefit. For professionals like physicians and surgeons, an own occupation clause is preferred.
This clause continues payment to a surgeon, if he cannot perform surgical operations, which is his regular occupation but if instead he can teach in a medical school. This type of disability policy provides continual income to the surgeon even if he takes on another occupation different from his current one .It therefore provides an additional layer of disability protection providing money to the surgeon, if he can teach in his regular field of expertise. Without an own occupation clause, no disability income would be paid to this surgeon, if he could engage in any type of occupation. His ability to teach would automatically disqualify him from receiving any disability income. Only purchase life and disability insurance from companies, which are AAA rated with respect to claim paying ability.

There is no point purchasing any amount of coverage at any price from a company if they will not pay when you need to be paid. This problem is particularly evident in the U.S. Therefore, investors beware!!!!!!!

MEDICAL INSURANCE

Be sure there is no duplication. If you have a good group medical insurance policy there is no need to purchase the same benefit again through your automobile insurance or private medical insurance policy. Do not waste your hard-earned money on duplicate benefits.

HOUSE INSURANCE.

Obtain at least a $1000 deductible policy. This will save you on premium costs in exchange for you being willing to personally pay the first one thousand dollar payment for loss due to any specific contingencies mentioned in your house insurance policy. Always obtain replacement cost coverage. Do not scrounge on this coverage. Replacement cost coverage enables you to get the insurance company to buy you a new TV, say, when your old TV gets destroyed in a house fire. Fire, contents and vandalism coverage's are important elements, which must be purchased as part of your house insurance policy.

PROFESSIONAL LIABILITY INSURANCE.

Secure at least 4-5 million dollars of liability coverage particularly if you are a doctor, dentist or lawyer. You may reduce your premium cost by assuming a higher deductible like $ 5000 or $ 10,000.

This means, you, as a professional, are responsible for the first $ 5000 or $10,000 respectively of costs in the event of a lawsuit involving legal and court costs and judgments levied against you.

ALL OTHER KINDS OF INSURANCE.
These should be normally considered at a later time depending on your circumstances and priorities. When a priority system is suggested for allocating your insurance payments, I do not suggest that you be without any essential coverage's you may require.

If sufficient dollars are not available to meet all your above needs do not panic. Continue to try to meet all essential needs through appropriate insurance coverage's --- lowering costs by shifting to lower cost alternative products can do this. Do make it a point not to miss important coverage's in one area because you have blown your budget in other areas. Remember balancing your needs and fulfilling all-important needs is a challenge you can meet successfully.

LEARN TO LIVE SIMPLE LIFE
If you are just getting started on the road to becoming a millionaire you might, on more than one occasion, be intimidated by the long journey ahead. You might feel that your income is quite small compared to the expenses you face in your daily life. This might make it difficult for you to visualize yourself reaching the goal of becoming a millionaire.

THE THREE WAYS OF GETTING RICH

There are three ways to get rich quickly:

1. Assuming your income falls in a predictable range; you just focus on spending less now. You cut down on unnecessary expenses, foregoing some of the pleasures of life now, assuring yourself that when you have accumulated a million dollars, that you can enjoy ten-fold the luxuries and comforts you have forsaken today. Think seriously about driving a smaller, secondhand, used car. Think and implement a spending plan, which cuts on your eating bills in restaurants. Take a packed lunch from home on a regular basis. Have simpler vacations. Enjoy two weeks barbecuing in a resort area close to home versus spending thousands of dollars on a vacation to Europe. Involve your wife or other significant partner and your children in all your savings and cost-cutting plans. After all, they too stand to benefit from your sacrifice today. Your fortune tomorrow is also their fortune and good luck tomorrow. Buy elegant clothes but only at year-end or other sales periods. Be creative in every way you can with respect to cutting down on personal, business and household costs. Make a monthly budget to track down all your expenses. Go through every expense with a fine toothcomb to see if you can reduce it or eliminate it. Another great way to build wealth is to pick a figure you can set aside from a savings perspective.

2. Let us say that you feel you can comfortably set aside 20 percent of your gross income into a savings program. If your family gross annual income is $50,000 per year, you now can save 20 percent of that, which is $10,000 per year. This amounts to approximately $833 per month. Just instruct the bank where you deposit your monthly income check to automatically deduct $833 every month from your checking account and transfer it into a money market account. This way, if you do not see the money as soon as it hits the bank you don't miss it nor are you tempted to spend it. Or better still employ the concept of a distance bank savings account. Open an account by mail in a bank in the next city close to yours. This account should have no attendant debit/credit cards/ATM facilities. It is simply a pure savings bank account. Instruct your bank to transfer $833 every month into this account. You would be surprised to see how quickly you accumulate wealth this way. You and you alone are responsible for your financial success. The sooner you start your savings program, and the larger the quantum of savings per month, the faster you can build your savings to a point where you can embark on a superior investment program.

II The second way of getting rich is to find a way of earning more income while capping your regular costs.

III The third and fastest way of getting rich is to earn more and spend less.

Illustration 7B

THE FASTEST WAY TO GET RICH

YOUR PRESENT FINANCIAL SITUATION IF YOU ARE A TYPICAL NORTH AMERICAN

ANNUAL COMBINED GROSS HOUSEHOLD FAMILY INCOME
(ASSUMING 2 INCOMES) _ _ _ _ $50,000

TOTAL ANNUAL HOUSEHOLD EXPENSES _ _ _ $51,500

YOU GO INTO DEBT TO THE TUNE OF _ _ | - $1,500 / year |

IN ORDER TO GET RICH
YOU HAVE 3 CHOICES

	CHOICE 1 Maintain Income cut costs	**CHOICE 2** increase Income maintain costs	**CHOICE 3** increase Income cut costs
INCOME	$50,000	$60,000	$60,000
COSTS	- $40,000	- $51,500	- $30,000
NET SAVINGS	+ $10,000	+ $8500	$30,000

Illustration 7B shares the financial experience of a typical American family. This family has an annual combined gross household income of $50,000 per year.

125

Their current situation and spending habits necessitate a total cost of $51,500 per year. They are, therefore, in the hole at the rate of $1500 per year. In order for them to get rich, they have three choices as outlined above. The illustration above shows the great power of increasing total income and simultaneously cutting costs. This affords this family the greatest opportunity to get rich quickly.

I would like to end this chapter with a true story. This story is of a successful life of a 29 year old engineer who migrated to Canada from South America. He left his country with $100 in his pocket. In four short years, he had moved into a big luxury home. He had also purchased good quality furniture and a nice car. He also shared his life with a beautiful woman. When I enquired into his sudden success he mentioned he saved 80 per cent of his take-home pay. I laughed at this notion, not believing a word of what he said.

He then proceeded to tell me how he did it:

1. There were two income streams in his household; one his and one of his spouse.

2. Their total take home pay was $42000 per year.

3. He lived in a basement apartment (before he bought his luxury home) and his total monthly expenses amounted to $700 per month.

4. His savings, therefore amounted to $42000-$8400 = $33600 per year.

5. In four years, he had saved $33600/year x4 yrs. = $134,400.

6. With $100,000 as a down payment, he bought the biggest house he could afford and qualify for (qualify for a mortgage). This gentleman's wife had bought into this wealth building process. They were both motivated and they achieved a success far beyond their wildest dreams.

In direct contrast to this successful couple's experience was a true story of another client of mine. This client was a very successful cardiologist. He earned $180,000 per year but spent $200,000 per year. He came to me with a very serious financial problem --- he was living way beyond his means and over a period of years was going down the debt hole pretty quickly.

This contrast was shocking. A poor South American immigrant earning $42,000 per year was far richer in four short years than an experienced cardiologist earning $180,000 per year.

The moral of this story is that it is not how much you earn that matters --- ultimately it is how much you keep that makes all the difference in wealth building over the long term. And if you have a burning desire and motivation to get rich, you will find ways of earning more and spending less no matter what your income is today.

It is not how much you earn today that is important --- what is far more important is how much you can cut your costs and get rich quick, as a direct result of such focused effort. With this, I rest my case on the effectiveness and long-term value of active cost-cutting strategies.

CHAPTER 10

Illustration 8

PUTTING ALL THE PIECES OF YOUR FINANCIAL PLAN TOGETHER

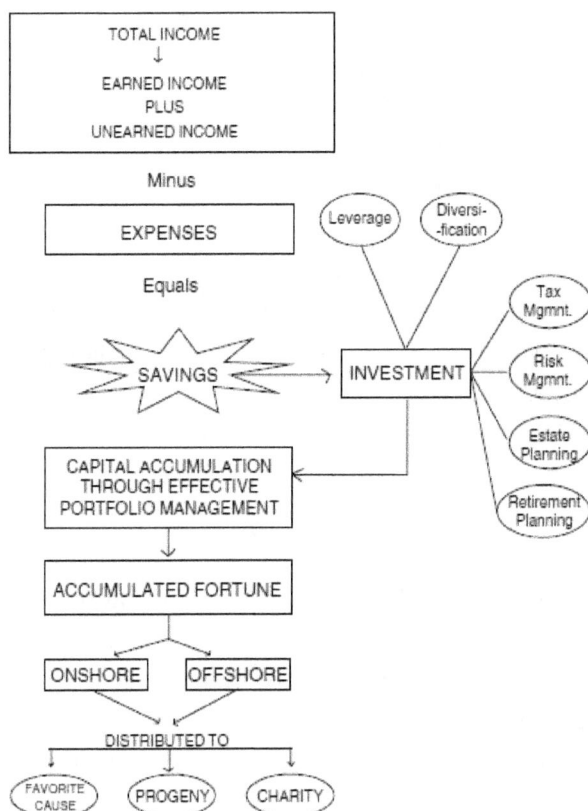

PUTTING ALL THE PIECES OF YOUR FINANCIAL PLAN TOGETHER

PRE-PLANNING PROCESS

Before you engage in efficient financial planning, certain initial steps must be adhered to --- these steps constitute the pre-planning process.

STEP ONE
Organization of personal and financial records.

Organizing your income and cost statements in budget form.

Preparation and analysis of personal income statement and personal balance sheet.

Tabulation and analysis of all types of debt.

Effective tax planning making maximum use of all eligible tax deductions.

Understanding and applying different types of tax benefits:

A. Tax deductible costs/expenses.

B Tax deferral schemes.

C. Shifting taxable income from higher income earner to lower income spouse and/or child.

D. Tax sheltered investments.

E. Matching capital gains and losses in any given year to reduce net taxes payable.

Setting and achieving savings objectives.

Setting and achieving investment objectives.

Setting and achieving educational funding objectives for children's education.

Reducing the cost of different types of insurance policies.

Effective estate planning for wealth preservation.

Annual financial review and check-up.

Step one outlined above deals with all the pre-planning required before an investor launches an effective financial plan for wealth accumulation. It is in the form of a checklist to jog your memory on the numerous things you, an investor, must do to make your financial plan for wealth accumulation a long-term success. Do note that getting rich is not merely a process of taking some risks and making it big in the stock or bond or currency market overnight. On the contrary, getting rich and staying rich is a long-term methodical process. You must stay motivated and focused and work constantly to preserve and enhance your wealth.

FINANCIAL PLANNING can be also visualized in the diagrammatic manner exhibited in Illustration 9.

Illustration 9

SIMPLIFIED EXPOSITION OF FINANCIAL PLANNING

```
                    SAVINGS GOALS
                        AND
                      STRATEGY

INVESTMENT GOALS                    ESTATE PLANNING
     AND                                  AND
   PLANNING                           DISTRIBUTION

INSURANCE GOALS                     RETIREMENT GOALS
     AND                                  AND
RISK MANAGEMENT                        PLANNING

                    TAXATION GOALS
                        AND
                    TAX PLANNING
```

SIMPLIFIED FINANCIAL PLANNING

I intend to share some simplified financial planning concepts and techniques, which will help you on your road to riches.

STEP 1. You must be fully aware of all your sources of income and all your expenses.

STEP 2. You must resolve to save!!!!!! Without a good consistent savings foundation you will do ZIPPO!!!! Cut all costs as much as possible. Live a super simple lifestyle! Save on all unnecessary insurance costs!

STEP 3. Once you have some seed capital in the form of savings, learn to set worthwhile investment goals. Do not invest one cent in the stock market till you can accept the following four conditions:

1. You must have at least a five-year time horizon. This is the minimum period of time you swear not to touch your principal. You also promise yourself you will not take it too much to heart if your principal drops 20 -25 percent in any given year but will hold steadfast to your original investment plan knowing in time you should get good results. You will also promise not to panic and sell any stock position when it is in a loss position short term.

2. The money that is invested in equities is normally money you will not require to draw upon for at least five years..A ten-year time frame will guarantee better probability of success in the stock market.

3. You can stomach a 30% DROP in value in an equity investment over any given year.

4. You have a tolerance of taking risks in the stock market and can sleep well at night even if you experience a short-term   loss.

You have the capacity to convince yourself that you have not lost any money in the stock market till you actually unload a position and sell it at a loss. You have the confidence that over longer periods of time, the stock market represents outstanding value for your investment from a risk-return perspective.

STEP 4. Do a careful review and cost benefit study of all insurance structures you are considering as important and pertinent in your personal risk situation. Remember your insurance priority list in the following order of priority: life insurance, disability insurance, medical, automobile, house, business/partnership, professional liability insurance. Be sure not to compromise on all necessary coverage's required today. If the budget is tight simply shift to lower cost product alternatives.

STEP 5. Do a detailed tax analysis both at the personal and corporate level to save every cent possible.

STEP 6. Do proper retirement planning analysis to ensure a decent and honorable retirement.

STEP 7. Plan your onshore and offshore fortune to ensure smooth tax-free intergenerational wealth transfer.

CHAPTER 11

PUTTING YOUR INVESTMENT PLAN TOGETHER

Your investment plan is probably the most important cornerstone of your future financial fortune. You are really trying to get rich as quickly as possible --- given your time, capital and risk tolerance constraints. This thrown in with market behavior will determine how fast your money grows and whether you can hang on to it. All the other steps and processes of financial planning merely exist to achieve your goal of getting rich.

Your savings objectives fulfill the first step of gathering some "liquid gold" (Capital). Cutting on insurance and tax costs can help you keep and grow this "liquid gold" faster. And good investment planning helps you keep accumulating your nest egg more rapidly and efficiently. Retirement planning and estate planning merely represent efficient ways of distributing and using your capital.

THE CENTRAL PURPOSE OF ALL FINANCIAL PLANNING IS TO ACCUMULATE A LOT OF MONEY SOUNDLY AND WISELY – therefore this entire chapter is devoted to this subject. Firstly, what are the avenues of investment available to you?

The broad basic categories of investments normally available to investors are:

1. Cash and money market instruments.

2. Bonds (Lending money for different periods of time to the government or corporations of different credit quality in exchange for a stream of income and re-payment of your loan at some fixed date in the future).

3. Stocks (Investment units in the stock of publicly or privately held companies normally listed on a stock exchange).

4. Managed bond funds (Investment companies who specialize in the investment of a pool of public capital in bonds of different qualities and durations).

5. Managed equity funds (Investment companies whose primary purpose is to use large chunks of public capital in investment of stocks of different companies with varying investment objectives).

6. Passive market linked equity and bond index funds (Investment companies, which invest on a passive basis in a benchmark of group of companies in a stock exchange --- investment being made either in stock issues or bond issues).

7. Offshore mutual funds. (Investment companies organized outside the U.S. whose purpose varies depending on investor's taste, e.g. companies specializing in sector investing, like computers or health care, companies engaged in geographical investing in different areas of the world, etcetera).

DETAILED EXPLANATION AND ANALYSIS OF PERSONAL INVESTMENT PLANNING

The first stage in your investment planning and decision making process is knowing:

1. What kind of annual return expectations you have overall for your investment portfolio.

2. How much liquidity or cash needs you may have in the short, mid and long term.

3. How much income you require on a regular and on an irregular basis from your investment portfolio, short-term, mid-term and long-term.

4. What is your appetite and tolerance for risk particularly during periods when your portfolio value is hammered by poor market conditions (bear periods) or during periods of intense market volatility.

5. What time frame you have for evaluating the success or failure of your investments.

Looking at the first issue above, if your overall expectation and demand from your portfolio is for any average annual return on investments over 12%, then this would involve a higher asset allocation of investments into the equity area. But this may not be practically feasible because you may require income and access to funds on a short-term basis. This creates the first major conflict in proper investment planning. Your return expectations on your investment may be high but you may not be capable of earning such returns if your need for cash and/or income are substantial and imminent.

Illustration 10

INVESTMENT POSSIBILITIES:
RISK - RETURN SCENARIOS

CASH	MONEY MARKET	BONDS	EQUITIES
IMMEDIATE ENCASHMENT	EASY TO ENCASH	MAYBE ENCASHED - HOWEVER PRINCIPAL LOSS PROBABILITY EXISTS ON PREMATURE ENCASHMENT	DIFFICULT TO ENCASH QUICKLY WITHOUT RISK OF PRINCIPAL LOSS
OPTION TO EARN MINIMAL INCOME	SLIGHTLY HIGHER INCOME POSSIBILITY THAN CASH	HIGHER INCOME THAN CASH OR MONEY MARKET	MINIMAL INCOME RETURN
VERY LOW RATE OF RETURN	LOW RATE OF RETURN	RELATIVELY HIGHER RATE OF RETURN	POTENTIALLY HIGHEST RATE OF RETURN LONG TERM
VERY LOW LEVEL OF CAPITAL RISK	SLIGHT DEFAULT RISK	VULNERABLE TO INTEREST RATE RISK AND DEFAULT RISK	TREMENDOUS PRICE VOLATILITY & CAPITAL RISK
CAPITAL MORE OR LESS GUARANTEED ON MATURITY	CAPITAL RELATIVELY SAFE	DEFAULT RISK BASED ON CREDIT RATING OF BORROWER	GREATEST OPPORTUNITY FOR LONG TERM CAPITAL GROWTH. NO CAPITAL GUARANTEE

One can view investment possibilities in the form of a continuum. Such possibilities are aptly illustrated above in Illustration 10. As one progresses from the cash type of investment to bonds and then to stocks one starts increasing risk. This acceptance of higher risk is accompanied by an expectation of higher return. The second issue of liquidity can severely damage the hope of creating large amounts of money in the future.

The very fact that you may require access to your invested capital for say, imminent education funding of your 18 year old child's university education may force you to commit your assets to shorter term investment vehicles like bank or money market accounts which normally pay lower rates of interest than bonds.

The third issue of income need can also damage your chance of accumulating a large nest egg quickly. Your income needs may force you to invest in short-term bonds, say, which will provide you with immediate income but will attract a lower probable rate of return than an investment in stocks over a long period of time. In addition to this you will also be assuming interest rate risk. If interest rates rise prior to maturity of your bond then, in the event of premature liquidation, you will be faced with a principal loss.

The fourth issue of your appetite and tolerance for risk is critical in determining the distribution in different asset classes with respect to your portfolio. If you feel you want to get rich fast and understand intellectually that large risks must be taken to achieve that result --- but then realize you cannot sleep well at night after taking such risks, then is it worth damaging your health and life in the pursuit of money? Maybe you need to consciously find ways of increasing your risk tolerance or failing that, downsizing your return expectations from your portfolio to maintain your health and life energy.

The fifth critical issue is the time frame you use in evaluating the success or failure of your investment. The markets seesaw on a regular basis and what appears to be a windfall at one point of time may become a disastrous failure when measured subsequently at another point of time when the markets have corrected and stock prices and bond prices have fallen appreciably.

How do you, as an investor, make sense of all this????? One day you are happy and ecstatic that your fortune is improving and another day you are down in the pits moaning of the ineffectiveness and inefficiency of your portfolio value. This is a real life problem, which must be faced positively by all investors if they are in the marketplace for several years. There is unfortunately no easy answer to this question. As an investor, you must realize that you are in capital markets (stock and bond markets) for the long haul. You must be emotionally prepared to accept some short-term setbacks. As long as you do not sell when markets are down out of either panic or emergency capital demands you are O.K. You must realize that you have not lost any capital till you actually unload a position. And that with time the values must come up. This patience, faith and long-term vision will help you deal with the gyrations in the markets. After all is said and done, it is still extremely difficult to emotionally accept a short-term setback.

If your emotional set-up does not allow you to bear this shock of lower portfolio values and you get ulcers and experience sleepless nights, it may be better for you to shift out of stocks and create a portfolio with cash and AAA bonds of varying durations and forget about earning a higher return. You may land up being less rich over the long term but you will be a lot happier. To sum up this issue, you must seriously ask yourself if you are willing to give your portfolio adequate time to grow. Too much money has been lost by serious investors who panicked or judged their portfolios too quickly and sold their positions at great losses resulting in wealth being corroded.

IN THE PRACTICAL WORLD, though, one has to survive financially first. This might involve allocating enough money in short term investments to meet with personal and family emergency needs like loss of a job, a serious illness in the family, etcetera. Then if you are planning to retire in the next few years, you may have to allocate funds to fund your retirement years, which might involve bond investments. Only after all immediate and short and mid-term needs are met and fulfilled can one plan and set aside money for serious long-term investments. Such investments involve the world of stocks and equities and represent the greatest long-term opportunity to make you rich.

Therefore, the process of building a quality investment portfolio for a new aspiring millionaire may involve first having adequate funds in cash, money market and bonds.

Once short and mid-term needs are met, then serious consideration must be made to allocating substantial sums to equity/stock investments. Only after basic needs are met can one move in the direction of equity investments.

PORTFOLIO COMPENSATION AND RISK DIVERSIFICATION

Portfolio compensation with respect to return expectations has a lot to do with the decision of distributing your wealth in different asset classes like cash, bonds and stocks. A higher amount of money allocation in stocks represents a more aggressive long-term position. This position not only gives an investor the greatest opportunity for capital gain in the future but also invites the greatest possibility of loss if the capital markets do not co-operate with your wishes for continual growth. Without taking this risk, there is no possibility of growth. But growth and gains are never guaranteed. The higher the cash and/or bond component in your portfolio, the more conservative an investor you are and the lower the potential for long term investment growth.

Illustration 11

DIFFERENT MODEL PORTFOLIOS

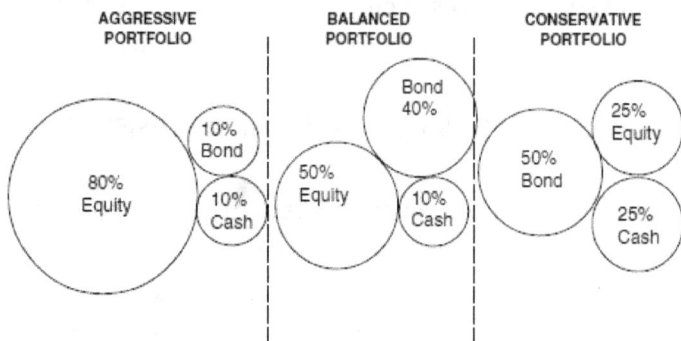

| AGGRESSIVE PORTFOLIO | BALANCED PORTFOLIO | CONSERVATIVE PORTFOLIO |

80% Equity
10% Bond
10% Cash

Bond 40%
50% Equity
10% Cash

50% Bond
25% Equity
25% Cash

As you can see, the aggressive portfolio in illustration 11 only has a 10% cash component. The balanced portfolio has 20% cash content, while the conservative portfolio has 25% cash content. Also, as you start increasing the equity component in your portfolio, you move progressively from a conservative portfolio to a balanced portfolio to an aggressive portfolio.

RISK DIVERSIFICATION is another principle, which must be followed for optimal capital growth in your investment portfolio. It is a good idea not to have all your eggs in one basket. Therefore spreading out your risk among different stocks and sectors and even geographical areas can smoothen out your returns. A very cheap and simple way to achieve good diversification in your portfolio is to invest in a mutual fund, which invests in an index like the Standard's and Poor 500 Stock index. This is a spread of investment on a capitalization weighted basis over the top 500 corporations in the U.S. This approach offers you good stock diversification.

CHAPTER 12

PLAN AND PROTECT AGAINST FUTURE THREATS TO YOUR FINANCIAL SECURITY

When it comes to the business of building your nest egg, it pays to look at investment matters from a panoramic point of view. An intelligent investor must look at all possible sources of attack on his wealth and guard against any possible intrusions and attachments to his wealth by predators. Here are some known and some not so well known threats to wealth formation and retention:

1. THREAT OF MARRIAGE BREAKDOWN --- PRE/POST NUPTIAL AGREEMENT

When one takes "marriage vows," one hardly thinks or dreams that the woman you vow to protect and love till "death do us apart" could suddenly become your worst enemy.

The national statistic of marriage in the U.S. boasts a 50% failure rate. You, therefore, on average, have a 50% chance of becoming a marriage casualty. One of the most effective ways of avoiding financial problems resulting from a marriage breakdown is to organize and sign a pre-nuptial or a post-nuptial marriage contract.

A pre-nuptial marriage contract specifies how individual assets brought into the marriage by each spouse and how assets acquired and built up during the marriage are to be split in the event of an irrevocable breakdown of the relationship. In practical terms, it is somewhat difficult to organize and sign a pre-nuptial contract. On one hand, you, the groom are promising to commit to your bride for a lifetime, while on the other hand you are demanding a signature on a piece of paper (called the pre-nuptial contract) demanding division of assets in the event of a marriage breakdown. It is as if you are planning your divorce before you consummate your marriage and uphold your marriage vows. However hard this might seem and however contradictory and strange this situation might be, a marriage contract protects both spouses and plans for a fair division of assets in the present when everything is happy rather than a later unknown and uncertain date. With respect to protection of your assets, proper pre-nuptial arrangements constitute a critical area of financial planning. When you are in love and everything is "kosher" is a good time to get the pre-nuptial contract out of the way. Just imagine trying to negotiate a financial severance package with an unhappy and angry spouse when the marriage either breaks down or is in bad shape. Many a family attorney will tell you just how difficult negotiations can be between two warring and unhappy spouses. Once a pre-nuptial marriage contract is properly drawn and signed in front of two lawyers who act as witnesses to the contract --- it becomes a valid and legally enforceable document.

Remember that each spouse must get independent legal advice pertaining to the ramifications and implications of the document each is purporting to sign --- otherwise the whole nuptial contract could come under legal attack. One spouse who has not been afforded the opportunity of independent legal counsel could easily take the position that she has been coerced into signing the nuptial contract and a judge could agree with this spouse and deem the contract null and void and unenforceable. Should you not have an opportunity of enjoying the protection and benefit of a pre-nuptial contract, then you must consider drawing and signing a post-nuptial contract. A post-nuptial marriage contract covers asset division between spouses in the same way as a pre-nuptial contract --- the only difference being that you draw up the agreement and sign it after your legal marriage (hence the term post-nuptial). In a post-nuptial contract, it is always advisable to also discuss child custody and child visitation arrangements. The number of fights and arguments regarding custody and child visitation are unbelievable.

2. THREAT OF BUSINESS PARTNER CONFLICT --- CHALLENGE OF PROPERLY DRAFTED PARTNERSHIP AGREEMENT

Should you be involved in a business partnership, a properly drafted partnership agreement is critical in protecting your business assets. Here are some of the agreements you simply must have:

A. BUY-SELL PARTNERSHIP AGREEMENT FUNDED WITH LIFE INSURANCE.

In its simplest form, this is a legal agreement between two or more partners in a business. In the event of premature death of one partner, the other partners buy-out his share or interest in the business at a pre-determined price (called the buy-out figure). This quantum of value equivalent to the buy-out price is funded and paid directly by the insurance company to the deceased partner's estate. In exchange the deceased partner's estate pledges to transfer his equity interest in the business to the surviving partners. The surviving partners pay the insurance premium cost as an incentive to purchase the deceased partner's share.

B. BUY-SELL DISABILITY PARTNERSHIP AGREEMENT
GUARANTEED AND FUNDED BY A
DISABILITY INSURANCE COMPANY

A long-term disability of a partner can wreak havoc on a business. Under this legal arrangement, if a disability strikes a partner in a business and prevents him from devoting his time and energy to the business, an insurance company pays a certain disability benefit to the disabled partner in the form of a regular income. In exchange for this continual income, the disabled partner agrees to sell his interest in the business to the surviving partners. The surviving partners pay the disability insurance premium costs to bind the coverage on the disabled partner.

3. THREAT OF ALL OTHER POTENTIAL LITIGATION
CIRCUMSTANCES
– LIABILITY COVERAGE REQUIREMENTS

This is one of the most challenging areas involving asset protection planning for investors. It is extremely hard to know who your next legal claimant is. This is particularly true for doctors, dentists, lawyers and financial planners who are constantly dispensing advice and relating with the solution of client problems.
There are only two foolproof ways to protect yourself:
Firstly, buy as much professional liability insurance that you can afford. Secondly, move a substantial portion of your assets offshore --- away from the jurisdiction and control of your home country.

147

3. BANKRUPTCY THREAT –
SETTING EFFECTIVE FINANCIAL &
LEGAL STRUCTURES PRIOR TO BANKRUPTCY.

This is also a very sensitive and challenging area of asset protection. In a situation involving personal bankruptcy, the investor must legally hand over all his assets worldwide to a trustee in bankruptcy. This trustee, for a fee, assumes the role of gathering, collating and documenting all investor assets and organizing to negotiate and pay all creditors with assets under his supervision and control. However, some investors decide to take the law in their own hands and transfer their assets offshore before a court action can seize any of their assets. Such actions are illegal and criminal in several jurisdictions and can get an investor in real trouble with the law in his country. This constitutes a fraudulent conveyance and can be punished pretty aggressively in a court of law. However, it is important to note that wealthy individuals who have transferred their assets systematically over a period of years prior to becoming bankrupt are in a somewhat stronger legal position than those who transfer assets to avoid creditors on the occurrence of personal or business bankruptcy.

However, in either case, you may be breaking the law by avoidance of your responsibility to disclose your assets in bankruptcy court. Do consult a bankruptcy lawyer to ascertain your rights and responsibilities.

SECTION 2

ADVANCED
INVESTMENT TECHNIQUES

CHAPTER 14

OVERALL RISK MANAGEMENT STRATEGY FOR THE ORDINARY INVESTOR

Now we start focusing on the real investment strategies guaranteed to help an investor save, grow and protect his wealth-----times are really challenging these days and it is critical that one clearly understands the components of good investing. Wherever one goes, one is bombarded with nonsensical yet persuasive looking ad pieces promising an investor untold wealth with little or no risk Authors have written and sold books to the unwitting and gullible investor on how to grow rich without risk. To understand this whole process of good investing one must start with a clear and unbiased understanding of risk management. This is the most important aspect of wealth building and not investment in stocks or balanced portfolios. With this in mind, the first chapter on investing starts with this lucid understanding of what risk is and how one needs to make this process of risk taking beneficial and successful for you, the investor.

WHAT IS RISK MANAGEMENT?

Wikipedia defines risk management as, "**Risk Management** is the identification, assessment, and prioritization of risks followed by coordinated and economical application of resources to minimize, monitor, and control the probability and/or impact of unfortunate events.[1] Risks can come from uncertainty in financial markets, project failures, legal liabilities, credit risk, accidents, natural causes and disasters as well as deliberate attacks from an adversary. Several risk management standards have been developed including the Project Management Institute, the National Institute of Science and Technology, actuarial societies, and ISO standards.[2][3] Methods, definitions and goals vary widely according to whether the risk management method is in the context of project management, security, engineering, industrial processes, financial portfolios, actuarial assessments, or public health and safety. For the most part, these methodologies consist of the following elements, performed, more or less, in the following order.

1. identify, characterize, and assess threats
2. assess the vulnerability of critical assets to specific threats
3. determine the risk (i.e. the expected consequences of specific types of attacks on specific assets)
4. identify ways to reduce those risks
5. prioritize risk reduction measures based on a strategy

The strategies to manage risk include transferring the risk to another party, avoiding the risk, reducing the negative effect of the risk, and accepting some or all of the consequences of a particular risk.

Now let us shift our attention to the concept of risk as it applies to the field of investments. The central concept of investment risk focuses around the probability of loss in any specific investment. If one is to assume a panoramic view of investments, one needs to go deeper into this issue. For example, why are you investing money? Most investors would say, without hesitation, that their sole purpose of conducting investments is to make a fat profit with as little risk as possible.

I would urge you to step back from whatever financial situation you may be in now and to look at your financial objectives from a broader point of view. A narrow point of view practiced by more than 99 per cent of the population is to make as much money as is possible with a minimal loss exposure in any specific investment. The broad view of investing is to look at investments with relationship to your Life's overall goals---- your Life is the most significant and important aspect of your existence; you must chart your territory in terms of meeting all your Life goals and not just a narrow goal of making as much money as possible in the least amount of time.

Two concepts can go a long way to understanding this approach. The first concept is the widely recognized portfolio approach. This approach calls for an integrated outlook to the growth of all your investments. Therefore you need to understand that whatever you own and owe becomes part of your total (and unique) composite investment picture. You grow richer or poorer not on the specific performance of a single investment but on the composite growth of everything you own and owe. So, in this big investment pie goes your house, your vacation property, your retirement funds, your stock options, your cars in addition to the stocks, bonds and commodities you possess. You grow richer or poorer by the overall performance of everything you have.

Do not forget your debts since they can sometimes accelerate your movement into the poverty zone---- something a lot of Americans have experienced in this great global financial and credit crisis.

If you find it difficult to map your financial portfolio on your own, an investment of a few hundred dollars with an accredited certified financial planner should help you map where you are now, portfolio-wise and whether you are growing richer or poorer by the day.

The second concept is a little more difficult to grasp. And this concept has to do with the prioritization process. By this I mean you need to, as an investor, figure out where your immediate priorities lie and then categorize these priorities on a scale of say, 1-10, with 1 being your most important priority and 10 the least. Then you allocate dollars to solving the problems you can to meet your most urgent needs first and then proceed with fulfilling as many of the other priorities at your income and cash flow will permit. It is such a national shame that most investment houses, stockbrokers and commercial banks have a totally narrow vision with respect to their customers' needs---- this is due to the fact that they push one or another product to maximize their commissions and revenues at the cost of the customer. They conspire individually and collectively to shift your attention and energy to the smaller picture of solving one specific financial problem, which is done at the expense of ignorance of your other more burning financial priorities.

In my humble opinion based on more than twenty years of field experience, the greatest immediate risks to your financial fortune hover around these three categories:

1. Financial loss, short and long-term to your family in the event of your premature death.
2. Massive financial loss to you personally if you cannot work short and/or long-term as a result of disability caused by illness or accident.

3. Loss caused by living too long and not having specific funds to finance your lifestyle during your retirement years.

Different investors view these three primary objectives or concerns at different priority levels. But for most of them their prioritization is focused on these three areas as primary investment areas.

On the other hand, there are a huge number of financially illiterate investors, who believe they are super-savvy. They look at various permutations and combinations to get rich quick. Really there are no rich quick schemes available to anyone. The promise of fast money is always accompanied by the risk of great loss. It is universally known that unless great risks are taken, it is impossible to get rich quick. Although, I am not denouncing the process of getting rich quick, I am advocating in this chapter on Risk Management, that the areas which have the greatest likelihood of inflicting a long term financial loss should be taken care of first and then after the investor has taken care of his basic needs, he should proceed to other avenues of investments.

STRATEGY FOR THE ORDINARY INVESTOR:
OVERALL RISK MANAGEMENT

Taking a cue from the earlier discussion, I would suggest the following investment plan:

PRIORITY 1 The provision of adequate disability insurance to cover at least 66.66%(two thirds) of your gross annual earned income, with residual disability provisions and a guaranteed insurability rider on policy.

PRIORITY 2

Adequate health insurance to support your medical, surgical and prescription medicine needs in the event of an unanticipated illness or accident.

PRIORITY 3

Provision of adequate life insurance to pay off all current debts and provide a guaranteed income stream of at least 75 per cent of your gross annual income to your spouse and loved ones.

PRIORITY 3

Proper investment planning to assure you at least 75% of your gross annual household income in your golden retirement age.

PRIORITY 4

Accumulation of at least six months of annual income in a bank or money market account for short term emergencies like funding a protracted period of unemployment.

PRIORITY 5

Adequate house, car and liability insurance to protect an investor's family in event of any catastrophic event.

PRIORITY 6

An investment plan which organized your financial life in the most tax-efficient manner.

PRIORITY 7

A long term blueprint to accumulate in excess of a million dollars of net investable assets----- this becomes a particularly valuable goal if you consciously desire independence and financial freedom.

PRIORITY 8

Creation of a superlative financial plan, which includes a process of orderly succession of assets through execution of wills, creation of estates and essential estate and succession planning.

UNDERSTANDING OF LIFE, DISABILITY, GROUP AND HEALTH INSURANCE

LIFE INSURANCE

Life insurance is one of the most highly misunderstood financial products in the world. This is due to two predominant reasons: firstly, universal fear of death accompanied by investor resistance to visualize his imminent death---- this leads to a conscious and sub-conscious rejection of any financial planning process assuming an investor's assumed demise.

Secondly, there is a lot of bad press and deservedly so on the fraudulent and dishonest representations by several producers representing life insurance, retirement and annuity products. To put this in perspective, it is a well established fact that approximately three percent of all insurance producers belong to the quintessential club of all, the Million Dollar Round Table. To me, qualifying for the Million Dollar Round Table was a measure of proficiency in customer service. The other 97% of non-Million dollar round table life insurance producers are a combination of hustlers, snake-oil salesmen and poorly educated and trained individuals, who will stoop to anything to sell a life insurance product.

You as an investor have to step away from this hype and view life insurance as simply a product which will replace dollars lost to your family in the event of your untimely and premature death. That is all that Life insurance represents--- a source of replacement income. Ask yourself, what would happen if you were no longer in the world tomorrow. Alright, I am not asking you a corny question, but challenging you to engage in a very serious enquiry concerning the financial state of your family without your income. How would your home mortgage be paid? Who would make the car and credit card payments every month? And where would the funds come from to finance your children's education? If an investor has any sense of obligation and love to his family, then life insurance is a must.

It is the investor's responsibly to scientifically calculate the exact amount of coverage required and to determine the combination of permanent and temporary (term insurance) coverage with a view to fulfilling his family's financial needs. But irrespective of this combination, the purchase of life insurance is a must if you have dependents and you love them.

DISABILITY INSURANCE

Disability insurance is another highly misunderstood financial product. It is basically a risk management tool to replace a wage earners income in the event of his inability to earn his regular flow of income as a result of unplanned disability. This disability could be caused by an unexpected and unplanned illness or accident.

In terms of need, what can be a greater need than one of a regular flow of income due to cash flow loss as a result of disability? The investor is cautioned to search and obtain reputable and efficient disability insurance products . Such products must be purchased by companies with superior claims paying abilities. A.M.Best and Company issues a credit rated list of companies, measured on their efficiencies in claims paying ability. Another important factor is that any policy purchased must be guaranteed renewable and non-cancellable. What this means is that the issuing insurance company must renew your policy at all times in the future and can never cancel your policy, irrespective of how many claims you may have made in the past.

HEALTH INSURANCE

It is a national shame and tragedy that more than 20 per cent of Americans have no health coverage of any kind whatsoever. This high number can be understood given the high cost of obtaining health coverage in the United States.

Health insurance, either to fully or partially cover your health and hospitalization needs is a must for every American. Imagine a scenario played out almost every day in America where a typical office worker suddenly gets afflicted by a disease---- he now has inadequate capital to pay all his medical bills. Bankruptcy becomes the only feasible option for such person.

Although it is understandable (from a financial perspective) that most self- employed or non- insured workers cannot pay to get a comprehensive health insurance policy, care should be taken to get some coverage. The long- term health insurance liability cap, where an insurer will provide you with, say $1 million dollars of health care costs can be particularly valuable in a situation of unanticipated medical emergency.

If money is the concern, get a policy with high deductibles to keep your costs low, but do not penny pinch on the long-term health cost guarantee by the insurer.

GROUP INSURANCE

Group life, health and retirement insurance usually are a bargain for most employees and an average investor is urged to get as much coverage as he needs and requires through his employer or association group plan.

CONCLUSION

In closing this chapter, an investor must realize that Living involves risks and such risks need to be faced positively and efficiently. Insurance is a smart way to shift the financial risk arising from illness, accident, death and retirement from the investor's plate to the ever beneficial hands of a solid and strong financial institution.

Focusing on the great dangers of falling sick or injured and/or dying prematurely are the first investment risks which need to be taken care of. Later, the longer term programs of growing rich apply. So many investors rush to make money at any cost to only find later that their health or liability situation wipes out whatever they have earned----this makes their long-term goal of getting rich impossible to maintain.

Therefore, first things first. Take care of your most important needs first; build a strong financial foundation and money and fame will come on its own.

There are no shortcuts to wealth and anyone promising you the Garden of Eden with no risks is lying and misrepresenting the whole successful investment story.

I have not met one person who got rich and stayed rich by taking short cuts.

Getting rich is a long-term proposition and success goes to them who are steady and patient. The tortoise always wins the race over the hare and you the investor must choose if you want to be the hare and make and lose your wealth in one lifetime or whether you choose to be a tortoise, who gradually but surely gets rich by first protecting himself and then gradually earns more and more money to fulfill his life dream of untold wealth and unlimited financial freedom.

It may be unfashionable to be a tortoise these days, but believe me that long run that is the only viable and successful way to go with your investment plans.

CHAPTER 15

INVESTMENT/ASSET ALLOCATION STRATEGIES FOR THE SMART INVESTOR

In the last chapter, the author discussed the importance of viewing your financial life in terms of a composite picture represented by your investment portfolio. This portfolio included all assets acquired in your life. It also represented all the debts taken out by an investor.

Most financial experts advocate the concept of smart asset allocation strategies. Before we get into this subject, let us look at the major asset classes in most investor's portfolios: these are cash and cash equivalents, bonds and stocks. The more sophisticated investors also hold gold and other precious metals, art and antiques, real estate, commodities and alternative investments. However, for an average investor there are four broad classes of investments, i.e. cash, bonds, real estate and stocks/equities. Most financial experts talk about different ways of breaking down your total portfolio into these four major asset classes. They propound that the younger you are and the greater number of income producing years, the higher the percentage of your portfolio should go to stock/equity investments, since you have the capacity to bear short term equity losses in exchange for better overall returns long term. This argument is quite plausible.

However, one needs to go deeper into this issue. My recommendation is and will always be first things first. If you are a novice investor and young and just starting out your Life your immediate priority should be to first save money. The purpose of saving money is to build a nest egg from which your financial life can be launched. The vital purpose of the savings process is to create a buffer of capital, which can be well utilized in the event of any short term emergency like employment when funds are required urgently. Once you have achieved a six month savings buffer you can then proceed to look at alternative investments.

My next piece of advice is for an investor to purchase a fine piece of real estate using banks capital as the predominant funding source. Irrespective of what anyone might say about real estate, nothing beats having a roof over your head, which one day can be yours free and clear. Being a renter is being at the mercy of your landlord and his financial future. Not to say about the constant bickering and interference from your landlord. From a tax perspective, purchasing a home is one to the greatest financial bargains today. In the United States, you even get to deduct the interest paid on the mortgage. Therefore, with a little money down you leverage a property which will hopefully grow to become yours in a short period of time, while enjoying complete control over your immediate living environment. And the Government gives you a tax break to boot.

As long as you do not sell your home in a panic and have a fifteen to twenty year view, you will have a great probability of creating wealth using someone else's capital.

Now that you have six months of money tucked away somewhere and a home which you can call yours you can start venturing into the world of bonds and equities.

Contrary to what a lot of individuals including financial experts indicate and teach, investing in equities is one of the riskiest financial exercises you can involve yourself in. This is due to the inherent volatility of stock markets. A great deal of the volatility is due to constant speculation by large banks, insurance companies and other institutional investors who want to make a quick buck. The easiest way to do this by disturbing the natural market price of a share. Investors going into this market with a very short term view invariably get burned. I have seen the smartest, most educated and financially literate investors get burnt big time, because they all want to make money quickly and fail to see the flip side of the investment picture, which is high risks, unpredictable volatility and a great probability of short term negative loss on their equity positions. My advice to anyone who wants to buy stocks is to have at least a ten to fifteen year time frame. This means that you never invest in the equity market if you do not have the patience or capacity to hang on to your investments for at least ten but preferably fifteen years. This approach will give you the best way of getting rich because you now have time on your side.

Now let us come to bonds. A bond is nothing but a certificate evidencing a loan from a borrower to you the investor. The bond specifies the interest rate, the maturity date of the loan and the e calculated yield to maturity. Bonds come in different flavors. Looking at the financial crisis of today, I would recommend that you do not buy any municipal bonds today, not even the AAA rated ones. Stay away from junior notes, which are second or third in line in the event of bankruptcy of the issuer. Do not buy bonds which are not investment grade. Since interest rates in the US are close to zero, this is a very bad time to buy long term bonds----- these bonds lose value as interest rates increase in the future. Given the financial crisis the only things which makes sense today is to buy floating rate bonds, these are bonds which pay you more interest as soon as market interest rates increase, so you do not take interest rate risk(unless interest rates decrease, which is very unlikely to happen now). Secondly, invest in investment grade bonds of shorter duration, probably not more than three years. This is because with the mad rush with which the US government is printing currency to support the various stimulus packages, interest rates and inflation are bound to increase in the future.

Now coming back to the asset allocation picture. If you are young and are earning a half decent income, after you have achieved your six-month nest egg and purchased a small home, then you may allocate aggressively in equities. Aga9in, my advice is not to buy individual equities but to buy an index fund.

The Vanguard S & P 500 index is a good starting point because it diversifies your investment in 500 of the top US companies and the costs of investment are very low. However, do not put a dime in any equity or equity fund, if you need that specific investment capital before ten years. So if you plan to get married in three years, you should not be putting that specific capital into an equity fund, hoping to get a handsome return. You could make a fast buck or lose brilliantly if the stock market tanks.

If you are approaching retirement then most of your funds should be in bond investments, since you have a need for retirement income.

Again, there is no hard and fast rule on how much percentage you should put in equities and bonds. The final decision is yours, the investors, based on what your cash flow needs are, what your level of risk tolerance is and how much time you have to ride out bad markets, because bad markets are found in both equity and bond investments.

CHAPTER 16

SUPERCHARGING YOUR RETIREMENT STRATEGY

Retirement marks an important phase in an individual's Life. It marks the end of a person's usual work career and the commencement of a life of rest and relaxation. One significant factor of concern is the total disappearance of earned income at this stage. The individual, who either chooses to retire or is forced out of his avocation now, needs to deal with the world on a new set of financial terms.

On one hand, a lot of his expenses are still in play but his earning capacity is severely diminished, even to zero earned income in many cases. But Life still goes on---- the car payments have to be made, the family (now probably just him and his wife) still want to go out on weekends and enjoy/pay for their annual vacations. However, the absence of earned income makes it tough going for most.

The second factor causing great uncertainty, stress and anxiety is the fact that one really does not know how long one will survive. So there is the added fear of outliving one's income.

In terms of retirement, then, an individual's past portfolio investment performance and prior retirement planning play a critical part in his ability to continue a stress free financial Life.

Financial experts have come out with some complicated mathematical models to determine how much money a family needs to accumulate to lead a stress free Life. However, in most cases the money is never enough to maintain the same style of Life as the family enjoyed when one or more breadwinners earned income and worked in their normal careers.

Since retirement is decades away for most younger aged investors, there is probably not enough consideration provided to developing an orderly accumulation plan to fund retirement needs. On the other hand, one may have the best financial advisors but if the assets inside the retirement portfolio go into a dive, one may have to postpone retirement. This is what has happened now with the current global financial and credit crisis. Numerous investors reaching their retirement age in 2008 or 2009 were counting on a certain quantum of assets, which when invested would generate a good income to fund their retiree lifestyle. With some equity and bond markets dipping by as much as 50 per cent in one year, investors now have no option but to continue working and deferring their retirement age. The other double whammy is that, due to the strains in the US financial crisis, the Treasury has been forced to reduce interest rates, to promote greater economic development. However, this lowering of general interest rates translates into lesser annual income for all individuals dependent on an income stream, particularly affecting retirees, who live off their retirement income in the process of sustaining their Lifestyle.

The end result of both these factors is most tragic and bears no relationship with the successful forward investment planning conducted by numerous investors.

Notwithstanding your success or lack of it in developing a good investment portfolio to fund your retirement needs here are some pointers of value to supercharge your retirement portfolio:

1. Put maximum contributions permissible into an IRA plan in the US. Such contributions provide a valuable tax deduction benefit and the interest on such investment grows without tax deduction till the proceeds are removed.

2. Participate aggressively to the maximum limits permissible in a group employer funded retirement plan.

3. Build a solid investment portfolio outside the normal retirement schemes to create a targeted amount of capital to finance your retirement.

4. Try to bring your debt level to zero prior to retirement.

5. Pay off the mortgage on the house prior to retirement.

6. Learn to live a simpler life and cut down on extraneous expenses not really required in a time of retirement.

7. Purchase and pay off completely a small vacation home to enjoy your retirement vacation time.

8. Plan on building a solid medical and health care insurance plan prior to retirement.

9. Organize one's affairs to pay off their life insurance policy (with respect to premium contributions) prior to retirement. In such an arrangement the insurance would continue post-retirement but premium payments would be suspended going forward while providing all the coverage/feature benefits of a permanent insurance program.

10. Organize your retirement medical care programs by taking maximum advantage of Medicare and Medicaid programs supported by the US Government.

11. Be sure that all retirement benefits are designated as joint and last survivor benefit, i.e. when one partner dies the other partner still gets retirement benefits.

12. Make all necessary estate planning arrangements prior to retirement to maximize tax-free movement of hard earned wealth and orderly distribution of assets.

13. Be sure that all necessary home, liability and car insurance are in place to protect against any unplanned exigencies.

14. Have a well thought out lifestyle on retirement. I have heard of so many individuals who have died early after starting their retirement because they simply did not plan their retirement time well.

CHAPTER 17

COLLEGE FUNDING STRATEGIES

In today's day and age, a college education marks the minimum qualification requirement to get a good job. However, with the great economic uncertainty in front of us and the need for greater doses of specialization, a post-graduate degree becomes even more important, both in terms of guaranteeing a good job and in terms of creating the skill/knowledge set for launching a successful business.

College funding strategies have all to do with how parents and/or their children plan to set aside, accumulate or borrow money to fulfill the child's educational financing needs. Needless to say, a simple strategy is to purchase a State college pre-funded plan. In such plans, available in selected states in the US, a parent puts a lump sum contribution which then provides the funding for the child's college education. The State then guarantees, that if the child goes to a state-sponsored educational institute/State University that the prefunding contribution suffices to pay for the four year education of the child.

In this instance, the State provided a guarantee that irrespective of the inflation rate at the age of admission of the child, there will be sufficient funding to pay for the university education. Such a program may cover only tuition or tuition and board.

Whichever way you view it, this process of prefunding a child's education is cheap and efficient. The only disadvantage to a child is that a State university degree is not accepted by employers as much as a degree from an Ivy League institution. However, in situations where parents cannot afford to pay the horrendous fees in Ivy League schools, affording a simple but decent State University education is a good way to go. A pre-funded State University education programs at least reduces some of the financing burdens of university education for the parent.

If a US parent earns under a certain amount of annual income, then there is broad eligibility for several loan packages sponsored by banks and US government. However, this is a complicated exercise and care must be taken to enlist the assistance of educational loan professionals to smoothen out the process and afford maximum loans for the child.

An even more important area in terms of educational funding is to first isolate what your child is interested in becoming when he grows up.

If your child is not totally sure of what he wants to do, it is always better to get him vocationally tested. This vocational testing process is easily available in any good institution. The testing process determines his strengths and weaknesses and looks at his native talent base and on this basis advocates consideration of one or more alternate career paths for the child. It is generally known that a child will always do better in an avocation for which he has the innate talent and skill.

FUNDING STRATEGIES FOR EDUCATION

One can fund university education through several different sources::
1. A prepaid education plan through the Government.

2. Loans available through different sources like the Stafford Loan Program.

3. Scholarships awarded directly from the University.

4. Individual funding through 529 College savings loans.

5. An investment plan set aside specifically to fund university education.

6. Life insurance proceeds available in the death of a parent or through funding afforded by a juvenile insurance policy. If a juvenile insurance policy is taken out, then a parent purchaser's an insured waiver in the policy. What the waiver does is most important.

This waiver automatically makes annual payments into the policy in the event of death or disability of the main breadwinner. So, if a parent does not live long enough to complete this insurance plan and dies prematurely, the insurance company continues to make the premium investments inside the policy on behalf of the child till the minor reaches university going age. This plan then becomes miraculously self-completing, irrespective of whether the main breadwinner in the family survives(or not) the child's university going age.

A SPECIAL LOOK AT IVY LEAGUE SCHOOLS

Getting your kid into an Ivy League school is next to impossible for any average working class American. Firstly, the annual tuitions are bound to break your back and secondly if you qualify there is the added burden to parent and/or child to pay for the loan after graduation. To me, the value of education in an Ivy League school is overhyped. If a child is provided a good broad university education and assisted in development of leadership, public speaking, debating and general organizational skills, then, in the long run this student can outperform and outrank any Ivy League graduate. The Ivy League degree only helps a kid get into a good corporation; it does not guarantee his future success. Although an Ivy league graduate can become a "hare" in the corporate world, the State University graduate although an initial "tortoise" has a greater potential to outperform this hare, due to superior job performance and leadership skills.

CHAPTER 18

HOUSE MORTGAGE, HOUSE REFINANCING & HOME INVESTMENT STRATEGIES

As part of your overall investment strategy, deep and prolonged consideration of the effects and impact of proper house mortgage decisions are critical. For most Americans, a home represents the greatest single investment of capital. It is a tragedy and shame to see so many Americans executing improper decisions regarding funding their mortgages.

Let us start our discussion with an understanding of what mortgages are. A mortgage is nothing but a "glorified" loan taken out from a lender, typically a bank----- the purpose of such loan is to fund the purchase of your home. Typically, a homeowner provides a down payment from his savings and takes a loan out for the balance of the purchase price of the home. However, this is where the simplicity ends. In order to maximize their revenues, the lenders have come up with an exotic range of mortgage options. They project and promote these schemes as being one creating additional opportunity and choice for the consumer------however such mortgage schemes are for the most part designed solely to line the pockets of the "fat and rich bankers".

To look at this issue from a historical perspective, one must see how the global financial crisis was caused through reckless, unethical (and criminal) granting and subsequent packaging of sub-prime loans. The banks knowingly knew that to increase their amount of loan able funds they would have to create a new mass market of buyers. They did this by exploiting, in many cases illegally, the sub-prime market. The subprime market represented a whole generation of subprime borrowers. Sub-prime in common finance parlance refers to "below average creditworthy borrowers". These were borrowers who had imperfect credit and/or low income levels with poor spending and saving habits. A bank, as a lender, now provided ability afforded to such poor credit risk taker to buy a house he could never afford let alone maintain in the future. The banks did this by offering low rate teaser loans. So, if the current market interest rates for a 15 year house mortgage was, say, 6 percent (like in the subprime days), the bank would offer the loan at say, 2 per cent. This made it possible for this subprime borrower to qualify and pay the monthly mortgage payments for a large home. These low teaser rates were for a very short period of time, typically one to two years. When the teaser rate expired, the bank reset the interest rate on the mortgage loan to a higher market based interest rate----- the subprime borrower could no longer afford the higher reset interest rate. This was due to the fact that the monthly mortgage payments now skyrocketed and created a cash flow crisis for this borrower.

This brings me to the first lesson in home mortgage financing. Never, ever elect an option to obtain a teaser loan, whether or not you are rich, middle class or poor. Only elect an option, which you could afford on your combined family salary. This would mean a ratio of no more than 35% of your gross annual household income. So, if you earn a combined annual family income of $60000, then the sum of $21000/year ($60,000 x 35%) is the maximum you can afford and this $21,000 includes your mortgage, property tax, maintenance and insurance costs. And do not forget to buy a group disability mortgage policy. What this policy will do is pay your mortgage on your home in the event of homeowners' sickness or injury, conditions which may cause you to leave your employment. If the group premium for such a mortgage disability policy is high, then consider obtaining a policy individually though an AAA claims paying insurance company. The extra premium is well worth the long-term security, which virtually assures you that the mortgage gets paid, irrespective of whether you are well or temporarily unemployed due to unanticipated sickness or injury. And be extremely sure that the disability plan covers all homeowners and not just the primary breadwinner. If you have a choice, elect a 15 year amortization period for your home mortgage.

THE INTEREST GAME AND WHY YOU SHOULD WORK
SMARTER THAN YOUR BANK

Interest is where your bank makes thousands and thousands of dollars from you and therefore it is crucial from a consumer's point of view, to pay off your mortgage as soon as possible. Now in the US you get mortgage relief by writing off your mortgage from your income earned. Still it is always advisable to pay off the mortgage early rather than late. Early mortgage payments create a great sense of security for a family---- a sense which cannot be replaced with anything else. If you have the comfort of knowing that the roof over your head is paid off, imagine how good you are going to feel if your boss forces you to take a 15 percent pay cut. Pay cuts are happening everywhere in this day and age of economic chaos and you must try to protect yourself wherever you can...

Coming back to the interest game, let me illustrate my point with a very simple example. Let us suppose you have a $100,000 mortgage amortized over 30 years at an interest rate of say, 6%. Your monthly payment will work out to approximately 525 dollars per month, which is around $ 6300 worth of payments in a year. Now, if you can financially afford to increase your monthly payments by around 125 dollars per month, you may be in a position to pay off your mortgage in a period of 15 years. You save yourself almost 6300/year x 15 years, i.e. $ 94,500 dollars in future payments by increasing your mortgage payments by 125 dollars per month.

And imagine the peace of mind which comes with knowing that you own the roof over your head.

HOUSE REFINANCING

Home refinancing is done due to several reasons:

1. Your home has appreciated in value and you want to pull out some of the equity to fund certain expenses. This is done through typically a home equity line of credit.

2. Your initial interest rate charged on our home loan is high and today's rates are lower, so you want to take advantage of the lower rates and you refinance your loan.

3. In terms of the Obama financial plan, homeowners faced with high mortgage payments may refinance the loan with a current interest rate. Given the low interest rate scenario in early 2009, this could save the average homeowner thousands of dollars.

Let us look at each of these options in details.

Option 1: Refinancing mortgage with a home equity line of credit

This is what brought the entire American financial system to its knees. In the heydays of 2001 to mid 2007, there was an unprecedented increase in real estate values.

Someone who had purchased a home in 2001 for, say, 100,000 dollars suddenly found the value of his home in 2007 at 200,000 dollars. Suddenly there was an increased value of 100,000 dollars for a person who had not done any appreciable work, save taking care and enjoying his home. The banks came up with a brilliant idea; why not allows this homeowner to tap this increased home equity? The banks would charge interest and make additional money on this additional mortgage loan and the homeowners would be happy. Thus started one of the longest periods of financial excess in the US. Homeowners started borrowing against their homes, withdrawing hundreds of thousands of dollars to buy more expensive cars, to procure new jewelry and among other things, engaging in more exotic vacations. And then, in 2007, the decline in real estate started leading ultimately to a total crash of home values. Homeowners, who had borrowed money on the strength of the increase financial value of their homes, suddenly found that there was no value left in their home. So millions of Americans found themselves with say, a $180,000 mortgage, which was comprised of an original $100,000 mortgage on which was added on an $ 80,000 home equity line----- in today's distressed real estate market, the home was valued at $100000. Therefore, you had a $ 180,000 loan supported by a home collateral value of $ 100,000. Now the homeowner had a negative worth of $80,000 in his home. What a tragic state of financial affair!!!! So you had this enormous debt accompanied with a negative equity situation triggered by falling real estate values.

This created the strongest blow to consumer confidence and the aftermath of this financial crash is well known to all of us. This brings us to the next rule of investing: Never, ever take a home equity line of credit unless you are engaging such funds in a productive investment. Never, ever borrow money from your home to finance personal expenses however noble they may appear.

Option 2

Refinancing can be undertaken when interest rates have dropped and you want to take advantage of lower interest rates. This seems a worthwhile strategy but an investor must look at all known and hidden costs of such a venture. First, ask your bank to give you, in writing, the costs of refinancing, then compare such costs to the benefits of lower interest costs. Do a present value calculation of both costs and benefits to see if it is an advantage to you or not. If it is an advantage, then refinance, otherwise stay away from his process.

Option 3

The new Obama administration has come up with a brilliant and socially conscious way to help the average American. Millions of Americans stand to lose their home since they have been locked in to high interest rates on their home mortgages.

The Obama administration is giving an average homeowner a once in a lifetime opportunity, to refinance the loan at a lower interest rate, with the US government picking up most of this tab of lower costs.

This is a great opportunity for an investor to lower these monthly costs ---- an opportunity which would not be ordinarily available since most mortgages have interest lock-in features for fixed time periods based on the original contract between the investor and the bank. This brilliant move by President Obama is designed to help save millions of American homes. Each and every American should take advantage of this new scheme.

HOME INVESTMENT STRATEGIES

Purchasing a home wisely is one of the best investments you can undertake. Irrespective of what you read in the press about the disadvantages of real estate investments, a home represents one the finest long-term investments in your portfolio.

Firstly, you can pay choose to pay rent for the rest of your life. The rent payments are usually made with after tax dollars. So, if you pay a rent of one thousand dollars per month and you are in the 35% tax bracket, you are in fact paying almost 1,400 dollars of pre-tax dollars per month for your condo or house rental. You have to earn 1,400 dollars and then pay tax at 35% on it, and the balance is left over to pay your rent, approximately. When you buy a house, you get a tax write-off on your income taxes.

Therefore, in terms of cash flow alone, paying 1,000 dollars a month rent is comparable to paying around 1400 dollars per month on a mortgage (including property taxes, maintenance and insurance). With 1,400 dollars per month, at today's 5.5% 30 year mortgage rate (approximate rate 8/1/09) you could leverage a property worth over a quarter of a million dollars!!!!!!

Although this sounds to be a simple situation it is not. Care must be taken not to exceed your affordability equation. This is 35% or better still, 30 % of your gross annual household income allocated to pay all mortgage costs. This is also followed by your assessment of career durability and the ability to continue maintaining this level of annual household income. Granted it is very difficult to project accurately your career longevity in these turbulent economic times----- nevertheless one must make some realistic projections of the ability to sustain your gross annual household income level well into the future.

The other factor is that with an investment in your house you can relatively control both the neighborhood you live in and secondly protect yourself from annual increases in rent(if you instead had rented instead of bought). You can talk to any renter you wish and you will invariably hear the horror stories involving unconscionable landlords, accompanied with inadequate maintenance of rented condos or houses; constant interference and harassment seems to be the order of the day. Do you really want to go through all this if you know that is cheaper and wiser long-term to buy a house?

And most importantly, a home affords the luxury of a superior long-term investment hedge against inflation. Although house values have fluctuated all across the map, it is a well known fact that in a long-term span comprising at the least a period of 25 years, you will always come out financially ahead owning as compared to renting ----- in the process you could create a financial nest egg over half million dollars by doing nothing(except investing your money in home ownership as compared to making our landlord rich by renting).

So then why is it that so many millions of Americans rent rather than own? Some of these reasons are:

1. A lack of financial understanding of the benefits of owning versus renting.
2. An inherited family lifestyle, where everyone known has rented properties as compared to owning them.
3. Fear is a great negative motivator. Numerous individuals are worried about additional risks taken by exposing themselves to loans of hundreds of thousands of dollars. The thoughts which go through their mind are: "What will happen if I cannot pay my mortgage tomorrow? What if my wife leaves me and I have less money to pay my mortgage? What if I am sick/ injured and cannot work and afford the mortgage?" These investors fail to understand that Financial Life is a risk and do not understand it is always better to take a calculated risk and buy something as compared to

renting, which is an emotional response to being overprotective and over fearful of their financial situation.

4. A lack of abundance is another factor. Numerous investors may not have available cash at the moment or may simply not have a saving habit to come up with cash down payments. This situation should be a challenge to an investor to change his financial habits; start saving money and get rich in the future. No change in financial habit translates to inaction and financial failure.

5. Poor credit history.

6. Instead of trying to improve their credit patterns, numerous investors continue spending indiscriminately and live beyond their means by not paying their bills on time. Unless they change their financial habits, they are doomed financially. And only they can change this sorry state of affairs.

In closing, appropriate house mortgage procurement strategies accompanied with aggressive refinancing moves by an investor backed by a good general foundation of values of home ownership, will help one build real wealth long-term by investing in a property of one's liking. You can enjoy and own a fine piece of real estate and get rich in the process. This is no pipe dream but a reality played out by successful American investors, day in and out.

CHAPTER 19

CREDIT CARD DEBT REDUCTION STRATEGIES

A credit card offers an opportunity for either great financial gain or for total financial ruination. It is sad that most Americans have used it to create massive and uncontrollable personal financial loss.

A credit card loan offers a worthwhile financial opportunity for an interest free short-term loan from an issuer, typically a bank. This is where its tangible benefit ends. The bank offers a loan based on a credit limit per credit card to a creditworthy customer. In order to increase their revenues and profits, numerous credit card issuers started offering cards to anyone and everyone. An average American had an opportunity of owning 10, 15 or 20 cards. So getting to an overall limit of 100,000 dollars credit was quite easy for most Americans with average to good credit, with average credit card limits ranging from 4,000 to 6,000 dollars per card.

The dangers of using credit cards are the horrendous interest rates charged by banks if the loan is not paid in time. Consumers racking up charges on their cards find themselves in a position where they simply cannot afford to pay interest let alone the principal of their loans on credit cards. Most banks charge interest rates of up to 30 percent. Since the usury laws have been abolished in the US, banks can charge whatever they want on unpaid loans.

Given this horrendous situation these are some simple rules on the use of credit cards.

1. Have as few credit cards as possible. You need to use credit to build a credit profile and score, therefore it is unwise not to use credit cards. Try to limit your purchase on them.

2. Instead of credit cards, use debit cards. A debit card is a card where purchases are funded directly through you savings account in a bank. There is absolutely no question of taking out a loan from anyone with a debit card---- therefore you pay no interest on any future outstanding loans and you are saved from future financial ruination.

3. Only use credit when you can pay off such credit card loans in time(usually 25 days from last billing cycle of creditor bank) or when you need capital for an investment. If you borrow from your credit card to fund an investment be sure that you can pay it off in 25 days----- if you need to fund a longer term business loan, you can apply for a commercial loan or utilize your home equity vide a home equity line of credit. The latter method results in major cost savings because the interest rates for such business loans if far less than the 24% or 30% interest you would pay if you financed this through the credit card program.

4. If you already owe thousands of dollars in loans on credit cards, then try to find some reasonable way of reducing interest costs. One way of doing this effectively and efficiently is to consider consolidating all loans and do the same by using a home equity line of credit. Your interest rate goes down dramatically and you have only one payment instead of five or six. You may go to a consumer debt service to look at ideas to restructure your debt.

5. If you are at a point in your Life when you cannot afford to pay any more credit card bills, consideration of bankruptcy is a possible option. However, bankruptcy is the worst option since it puts your credit score at an extremely low level for several years and it also puts your other assets at risk.

In closing, a smart investor will avoid credit cards as much as possible. Credit cards represent the worst way of financing capital and the only beneficiaries of their use are the big, fat profitable banks. You do not exist to service the banks and make them rich. Use of credit judiciously is advised--- the concept of judiciousness involves, for example, the prudential use of capital exercised in taking out a loan to buy a house or condo, use of capital through credit cards for super-short business investments or by simple use of credit card when 100 percent of the balance is paid off in time, avoiding any interest charges.

You are now playing the same game as your bank, except that you are smarter than them. You are using the bank's money for free, as long as you repay the loan in the stipulated period of time. And do not forget to take advantage of all the freebies associated with some credit cards, like a certain percentage back on gas and retail purchases and frequent flier points.

Credit card use must be wise and efficient to make it valuable for a consumer. However, in most cases, we see an average American spending beyond his means, financing such excesses through indiscriminate use of credit cards. We are now experiencing a loss of hundreds of millions of dollars for the banks with respect to rising credit card delinquencies---- these are the same commercial banks, which were hungry and greed in encouraging credit card use and now have got caught with their pants down. Loose credit standards resulting in arbitrary provision of credit have amounted to great suffering and pain to consumers.

CHAPTER 20

COMPREHENSIVE INSURANCE STRATEGIES WITH PRIORITIZATION OBJECTIVES

As illustrated earlier, risk management is the most critical component of investment portfolio management. Insurance is a complementary term for risk management. So let us look at what the risks are in terms of an average investor.

Risk basically indicates a potential for loss and we now need to look at all areas involving potential capital loss. Capital loss does not only entail an understanding of loss of capital from inside an investment portfolio---- it also must take into consideration what the risk is in producing capital.

There are only two ways of making money:

1) Money makes money. This is the area of unearned income, where capital suitably invested in gold, property, stock, bonds and businesses generate a flow of income. Money making money is capital employed suitably to create new money (income).

2) People making money. This is the productive enterprise of people who generate income through employment, business and professional practice.

Although a lot of literature and attention is given to active and inactive strategic portfolio risk management, very little thought has been given to the effects of an individual's productive capacity. It is a tragedy that you try to protect the golden eggs and not the golden chicken which produces such eggs. Early on in this book an illustration was given about a golden chicken which had a remarkable and unique capacity to lay golden eggs. Then a question had been posed to the investor, "If you had the capacity of keeping one and not the other, which one would you choose? The golden chicken or the golden eggs." Almost everyone would think of protecting the chicken, since this bird had a remarkable capacity of producing multiple golden eggs.

However, in real Life, we investors demonstrate the exact opposite thinking. Let me explain: "Does anyone not have car insurance, property (home/condo) insurance? Most people own car and property insurance---- this is a fact. And do most people not have disability and life insurance? Not really. Life insurance is looked down by the general populace and how many people really comprehend the benefits of disability insurance? I would say, very few."

The car and property refer to the golden eggs. The disability and life insurance deal with the golden chicken. What is most important is to protect the ability to earn income (golden eggs). You are the golden chicken. Disability insurance assures the fruits of the effort of an individual in the form of income continuance even when the investor (golden chicken) is unable to do so as a result of sickness or accident.

Life insurance provides a never ending stream income to family and creditors in the event of the breadwinner (golden chicken) not being able to continue earning income as a result of premature death.

This brings me to the prioritization issue. This is that more attention and priority must be given to disability and life insurance and less to car and property insurance. This advice does not mean that you must not secure car and property insurance. Merely that more of your premium funds available for insurance investments should find themselves directed to disability and life insurance.

In terms of further prioritization, one is invariably faced with the shortage of funds. No one has adequate money, irrespective of how rich they are, to provide for each and every insurance need. Therefore, there must be a budget established upfront of the total amount of capital available for all your risk management needs. Say, for example, you are earning 40,000 dollars per year and have set a total insurance/risk management budget of 4,000 dollars per year. Then you need to prioritize the amount of premium to be channeled into your various risk management/insurance needs. For most investors, I would suggest the following prioritization in order of importance:

1. Disability insurance. If you can buy group disability insurance with all the right features, this would save you a lot of money.

2. Life insurance: First proceed to buy as much group life insurance you can. Then purchase as much association life insurance as you can, from groups like the AARP, your credit card company, etc.

The rates for group life coverage are low. Then purchase a variable universal life policy for the balance coverage required. For guidelines on how much insurance coverage is essential, please refer to my earlier chapter on this subject.

3. Purchase a liability insurance policy for at least a million dollars. You can buy an umbrella liability insurance policy for a relatively modest sum of money.

4. Now you can purchase automobile insurance with high deductibles but substantial liability coverage.

5. Next purchase condo/house insurance with higher deductibles to save on premium.

In terms of protecting your portfolio, a variety of hedge and alternative investment strategies can be employed. Detailed discussions of these strategies are beyond the scope of this book. A good certified financial planner, preferably with a CFA degree, will be able to assist you in setting up novel protective strategies for your investment portfolio.

In closing, mention must be made of the fact that many people are "insurance poor". By this I mean, they have so much insurance that they feel poor at the end of the premium paying exercise. However, a lot of the premium is wasted on the wrong type of insurance and the wrong type of policy. In numerous cases, this is because of poor advice from an insurance agent and/or financial planner.

An investor must take the time and effort to educate himself by taking on line investment courses from reputable universities and learning houses; read the Wall Street Journal and keep on top of cutting edge investment ideas. It is the smarter, better informed investor who earns more, keeps more and invests in the right risk management/insurance vehicles.

CHAPTER 21

SAVINGS STRATEGIES FOR WEALTH GENERATION

Savings constitutes the first and most important step in wealth creation. It does not matter how much you earn in your lifetime---- it's how much you save from what you earn which makes the difference between success and failure in Financial Life. I had earlier on shared a true story of an immigrant client of mine, who had arrived on the shores of Canada with no money---- he, however, possessed a unique and burning desire to get rich. I shared his successful result of being able to save more than 65% of his gross income for several years. This helped him invest the new found capital in real estate, which ensured he became very wealthy in his middle years. So, my exhortation to every reader of this book is to forget all the fancy investment ideas you hear about every day. Stop envying the millionaires around you who get publicized on TV, radio and press. Look at yourself as the most important investment goal. Save at least forty per cent of everything you make. If you cannot reach this goal, then save, at a minimum, twenty per cent of everything you earn. And keep saving this amount as a percentage of your income for the rest of your life. Then forget about everything. Just invest the money in very simple investments, having enough set aside separately for short term emergencies. You will surely get rich one day.

In terms of savings strategies, the less that is said the better. The more complicated we make this subject, the worse off we become, results wise.

To follow a wealth building pattern, which defies the ups and downs of the economic cycle, you must go against the tide and commit to saving money regularly and consistently. Provide a home of your own to your loved ones. Buy a home and never rent one. Set up a well allocated asset investment plan. Have enough insurance in a prioritization form to protect your needs of tomorrow. And don't get sidetracked by advice from the numerous bogus investment gurus.

Live simply, save consistently and be patient in terms of results expectation. Sooner, than later, you will grow rich and have enough to live a comfortable and happy retirement Life.

CHAPTER 22

SMALL BUSINESS WEALTH CREATION STRATEGIES

It is quite a challenge to get rich quickly in America. Given the nature of the unique American capitalistic system, the business world here expresses itself as a veritable," dog-eat-dog" mentality. An American entrepreneur takes all the risks, lays out his hard earned capital for a presumably good business idea and then puts in the time and effort in his new business, knowing there are more chances that he will fail then not. In fact, there exists a 95% probability of failure in the first ten years of his business.

So, anyone involving himself in a business venture should take a long and hard look at all internal and external financial circumstances before jumping into a new business. Having said that, what opportunities exist to create wealth in the small business field for an average investor? Thousands of books have been written on this subject. I would now like to summarize, in very simplistic form, the main elements of wealth creation success in small business:

1. Have a well thought out strategic plan. Why are you in your chosen business? Who do you plan to serve? What unique features do your product or service has which is superior to competition in very way? How do you visualize your process of serving your new   clients?

These are some of the more important questions you need to ask yourself before you even consider a specific business from a capital investment point of view.

2. Have a well thought out written business plan. This plan should take into account all the ramifications of cash flow planning, budgetary planning, marketing and sales planning, competitive planning and a host of other factors.

3. A well thought out marketing strategy and marketing plan. Marketing forms the vital link to wealth creation in your business. Therefore, detailed marketing strategy, tactics and plans need to be assembled first. Such a plan must involve a study of break-even points, month-to-month projected sales and a translation of sales into profits and break-even points.

4. An understanding of the major players in your business in terms of either equity talent (partners) or hired help (professional employees). What sub-set of skills and talents are you bringing to the table and what makes your offering superior to the other competitors in your business?

5. Provision of adequate risk management measures to protect your growing business are critical. This involves adding group insurance, in addition to inclusion of a properly funded partnership insurance structure and good disability insurance.

6. An honest understanding of how long you can last if your business does not take off. You need to know how long your financial resources will survive in the event of a failure of the business...

7. Proper exit strategies. How do you plan for any fall out between the partners? Or with any of your key employees? What is your back up plan for the business if it does not work? Can you adapt/transform the business to something else? What is your exit strategy?

8. Proper motivational training is a key consideration conducive to business success. Have you exercised and delivered the best training programs for your employees? Do you have state-of-the-art computer systems to guarantee business excellence? And how well are you publicizing the business to your target market?

9. How does your newly formed business sit in when viewed with the rest of your investment portfolio? Have you allocated your business assets optimally and efficiently so that you see the business as only part of your bigger investment portfolio?

Or are you like most entrepreneurs who bet the house on a single business venture, never to wake up in fine shape once that business collapses?

These are a few of the critical factors for wealth creation in your business. It is by no means an exhaustive list but a starting point for business excellence and success.

THIS PAGE LEFT INTENTIONALLY BLANK

SECTION 3

PERSONAL GROWTH STRATEGIES FOR WEALTH ACCELERATION

CHAPTER 23

SELF-DEVELOPMENT STRATEGIES

Most investors fail to realize that every aspect of their Life is interconnected. Let me elaborate. Your business and financial Life is intimately connected with your personal Life. So many investors believe that the real key to business success rests in a primary focus on business activities, which generate money. In the process of achieving their financial results, they fail to pay heed to their personal needs and desires.

And what are such personal needs and/or desires? Personal needs operate on the following levels:

1. Physical needs, e.g. the need for exercise, good sleep, relaxation and positive physical energy.

2. Mental needs, e.g. the need for a sense of comfort and peace in your surroundings and in your variegated relationships with people, ideas and nature including the special energy fields (circumstances) around you.

3. Emotional needs, e.g. the need to be loved, to share the fruits of your efforts with the ones close and dear to you and the feeling of complete emotional comfort with your goals, business and external activities.

4. Spiritual needs----this is by far the most important and highly ignored area of personal development. Spiritual needs deal with your connection to an omnipotent and powerful Life force around you. Alignment with this force makes energy channelization easy and assists you in effortlessly getting what you want.

The process of creating and sustaining self-development strategies calls for a total understanding of all these forces around you and your ability to harness them to work in your favor. This chapter and the next few will provide some starting pointers to you in your quest to not only be rich and successful, but to enjoy the journey called Life. The role of self-development is to assist you in getting from point A to point B in a happy, quite and relaxed manner. You must enjoy the fruits of your hard work; otherwise, what is the point of this journey called Life? And this enjoyment is not just at the end of attainment of a worthwhile goal but during the real tough and challenging process of acquiring positive results in your Financial Life. I have seen numerous clients, who were very wealthy, but at the same time exhibited negative polarity----- these rich individuals were the most obnoxious, unhappy people I had ever met in my Life. These individuals served to point out what the lack of meaningful self-development strategies entailed. Money without a deeper purpose has no value at all.

Here were rich people who had lost the way. Their financial abundance was all that they possessed; their personal life was filled with doubts, anger and jealousy. This is exactly the road I do not want the reader to take. Believe me, it is very easy to turn self-introverted and angry and fearful when you possess a lot of material wealth. These few chapters talk about balance, love and happiness as you strive to get what you want. The author wants you to consider a balance and integration in everything you do. Wealth without physical, emotional, mental and spiritual balance is a curse and it is the author's hope and prayer that you experiment with some of the ideas in this and following chapters to enhance the level of peace in your total Life. You must see material wealth as just one part of the overall wealth of Life if you are to stand any chance of making a quantum Leap to happiness.

Life is truly a gift from the Lord!!!! Enjoy it in every way possible. Count your blessings for being alive and awake every morning: be grateful for all the good and loving relationships around you and be most happy to live in North America, one of the most beautiful and exciting places in the world.

The details of self-actualization and self-actualization processes are beyond the scope of this book. Detailed information can be obtained by reading the author's book, "You have it all now---your Life is yours to truly discover and enjoy." It can be ordered without fuss and fanfare at the author's private corporate website, www.pioneer-communication.com

CHAPTER 24

PERSONAL HEALTH AND WELLBEING STRATEGIES

Health is a crucial part of your overall Success development. It is intimately linked with your overall financial Life. An investor needs the physical energy to operate in the external world. He needs the physical stamina and persistence to move on, while facing a lot of flak and negative resistance as he moves from point A to point B in his elusive search for Success.

Health is a complex subject----- however, it suffices to say that an investor must be fit and healthy; he must also keep a physically vital and alive organism by performing regular annual physicals and eat nutritious foods in addition to maintaining an optimum weight. Regular exercise is also crucial. Any kind of strength development and maintenance exercise would do, but the cardiovascular ones like walking, jogging are the most effective and productive. Rowing is a particularly valuable cardiovascular tonic. As a viable alternative, I recommend brisk walking to anyone. It gives you a chance to be quiet and enjoy nature while operating on a deeper meditative energy level. Any exercise is good as long as it is done consistently for at least a forty-five minute stretch.

On the other side of the coin, if you do not exercise and stay fit, you will sooner or later lack the energy to fulfill your Life work. I have seen, in numerous cases, that individuals who have well laid plans of business are simply not able to achieve their goals due to poor health.

CHAPTER 25

SPIRITUAL STRATEGIES FOR A
HAPPIER AND MORE BALANCED LIFE

Spirituality is one of the most misunderstood areas of Existence. Most individuals mistakenly associate spirituality with religion when Spirituality has nothing to do with it.

Spirituality encompasses a broad and complete acceptance of all Life energies around you. Spirituality deals with a total awareness of all the Energies around you. It challenges you to understand the nature and scope of your relationships with others, with things and ideas and with nature. In fact, spirituality represents the total embodiment of Life.

Due to the dearth of proper information and the general level of ignorance, investors are not able to tap into this powerful Source of Energy. The author is not suggesting you discard whatever religion and values you have. He is merely suggesting that in addition to whatever religious choices you exercise now, that you consider opening yourself to "New Age" choices.

Meditation was discovered in India and China, thousands of years back. Gautama Buddha, after whom a whole new religion has been created (Buddhism), was one of the earliest meditators known to mankind.

Although it is not the purpose of this book to promote Buddhism or any other religion, or get into the devious act of comparing religions, it suffices to say that you can tap the Energy of Intensive Meditation to reach your Life goals. Meditation is a process of detachment from thoughts, distractions and pulls and demands from the outside. It is a process of suspension of external Life. The Mind is a powerful source and it creates and sustains Human Life. It does so by creating external demands, though needs, wants and other desires. In the process of this External Life, one loses touch with ones innermost self. Being quiet and in a meditative stance clears the Mind and allows one to be reconnected with one's inner balance and Energy.

There are numerous good books on Meditation. Some of the best and most effective are, "Beyond the Mind," by Dada. The author would be glad to send you the book if you are seriously interested in using the power of meditation in advancing your Life. I would strongly suggest you read books by J. Krishnamurthy, Dada and others to help you open up your Life to possibilities for happiness. Happiness and wealth are synonymous factors and one can be both happy and rich. It is the author's suggestion to challenge the reader to open his Life to the limitless possibilities of Inner and External Wealth.

CHAPTER 26

PERSONAL RELATIONSHIP STRATEGIES FOR A CONFLICT-FREE LIFE IN TOUGH TIMES

Personal Relationships form a crucial part of the overall integration of Life. In all relationships, conflicts arise as a necessity. The reason for such conflicts is the clash between different mental, emotional and physical expectations. A human being is a complex ball of numerous wants, needs, hidden desires and expectations. When two human beings come together, whether to procreate, love or do business there is of necessity a clash between two different energy levels. Each human wants something from the other, whether it be love, companionship, entertainment or an opportunity to make money. The other human has their own conscious and unconscious list of desires and expectations. There is in fact a give and take between two or more humans, whether it is on a personal or business level. And when one human feels he is not getting enough in exchange for his investment of time and energy, there is a new demand placed on the other, which creates a conflict position.

Needless to say, one must accept the fact that there will always be a push and pull in any relationship, whether it is intimate or whether it is superficial or a business relationship.

However, when relationships get so warped that the conflict level increases dramatically with very little attendant happiness, then an individual needs to ask himself whether it is really worth staying in it.

It is a well known fact that the richest and most successful businesspeople have a strong and loving emotional bond in their Life. It is rare, that an individual can carry on successfully without any external emotional or love bonds. So, what does this relationship conflict level have to do with financial success? I believe it has everything to do with it. In the current global financial turmoil, numerous households have at least one member, who has lost a job or has lost income due to downsizing of time or wage. In such circumstance there is a massive pressure on the family unit to sustain itself because although the family income has reduced, the expenses have still stayed the same. Such dire economic circumstances cause the need for a reexamination of the relationship and solidarity moving forward.

In many cases, such solidarity is missing with each partner getting frustrated and angry that they cannot get the material things they want, due to a loss of income at the household level. In some instances, this adversity can severely test the strength of a relationship. It is critical to sit with your partner or significant other, to clarify why you are in the relationship in the first place and to reinforce the fact that this economic downturn will at most be a passing phase. If however instead of this, you get a continual barrage of abuse and anger and discomfort, one may have to consider leaving a spouse or significant other.

In this case, one must view this as a blessing---- maybe this dire economic circumstance has shown that there is a fundamental lack of trust and confidence in the relationship and one must exit this situation for the sake of one's own sanity and peace.

The economic crisis has created considerable harm and pain in most American households and it is my sincere hope that families see this as an opportunity to come together and enjoy their time together, thereby reducing the stress and increasing the Love. Because Love is what Life is all about. The family unit is designed to be a bastion of emotional security, and if that is not available in the relationship then why have it in the first place? Why continue with the pain and stress? Surely there are easier, more productive ways to live.

CHAPTER 27

SUMMARY

This book marks the final installment of the classic three book series entitled, "Quantum Crisis." While Quantum Crisis 1 deals with the history of past world financial crises, Quantum Crisis II explores in detail the current credit and financial crisis of 2007-2009. Quantum Crisis III(this publication) now shifts into high gear. It takes from the knowledge of the last two related publications, to provide prescriptive investment advice to interested readers.

This publication starts with an overview of the current credit and financial crisis. It then discusses basic investment strategies crucial for financial success. Savings, investments, risk management, estate planning and cost cutting strategies all work together to develop a broadly successful and cohesive investment portfolio. Now the publication explores advanced investment strategies. This study includes an understanding of complex financial planning. Advanced retirement strategies, credit card interest reduction strategies and home financing alternatives, are among other subjects discussed.

This book ends with exhorting the reader to integrate all aspect of his Life together. It does this by proposing that a well integrated physical, mental, emotional and spiritual Life will result in greater Success for the investor with more happiness and less effort.

And is this not what Life is all about? Less work and more happiness. More coordination and integration with maximum productivity.

More fun and happiness through this marvelous journey called Life ----such Life being filled with Quantum Success, Peace and Prosperity.

CHAPTER 28

CONCLUSION

This financial crisis is like none since the Great Depression. Millions of Americans got spoilt in the yesteryears starting in 2001. This was the time when real estate values starting appreciating in the US. With more money on their hands through indirect wealth formation through increased real estate values and a soaring stock market, Americans started spending money like there was no tomorrow.

Tapping into home equity and selling portions of their stock portfolio, they withdrew hundreds of thousands of dollars from their portfolio. They splurged on exotic foreign vacations, on dresses and paraphernalia at the upscale shopping boutiques, on fancy cars and unbelievable Life styles. But sooner or later this party had to get over. And when the hangover effect hit home it was devastating. In a flash of a second, it was all gone. Suddenly there was nothing but bad news in the air. Decimated stock markets, shrinking home values and rising mortgage delinquencies were the order of the day. And the average American was shaken up from his sleep.

Suddenly there was more emphasis on personal values and family relationships. The tough times emphasized that family, love and good relationships were more important than the never ending chase for more and more material wealth and gratification.

But fundamentally, this economic mishap changed the nature of relationships between people. It caused people to question their undying adulation of their money relationship and it made them look at more fundamental aspects of Life like Love, good family relationships and a simpler Lifestyle.

Maybe this was an omen from the Almighty to challenge the American to live a simpler, more streamlined Life. And this change has already started. The national savings rate in the US has soared. People are paying off more of their outstanding credit card balances. And families are spending more time with themselves cherishing the values of children and simple things like a barbeque party on a park as compared to a vacation in an exotic overseas location. This crisis has transformed for ever fundamental human relationships.

On one hand there has been great pain and discordance with families splitting up and individuals falling sick as a lack of adjustment capacity to cope with the new financial landscape. On the other hand, there is a new start towards good and more valuable human interaction--- the start of more Love, Balance and Simplicity. The author truly hopes you have learnt positively from this most devastating economic and financial crisis.

Live happier, live simpler and place more emphasis on personal relationships ---- these are more important that all the money in the world!!!!!

CONSULTATIVE APPENDIX

"QUANTUM CRISIS I"
-"ORIGIN OF GLOBAL FINANCIAL CRISES "

TABLE OF CONTENTS

PART ONE: THE BACKGROUND HISTORY OF PAST FINANCIAL CRISES

CHAPTER 6
THE DUTCH TULIP BUBBLE OF 1636

CHAPTER 7
THE SOUTH SEA BUBBLE OF 1720

CHAPTER 8
THE FLORIDA REAL ESTATE BUBBLE OF 1926

CHAPTER 9
THE GREAT DEPRESSION

CHAPTER 10
THE REAL ESTATE AND STOCK MARKET BUBBLE
IN JAPAN 1985-1989

CHAPTER 11
THE REAL ESTATE & STOCK MARKET BUBBLE IN
SCANDINAVIA 1985-1989

CHAPTER 12
THE ASIAN FINANCIAL CRISIS OF 1997

CHAPTER 13
THE NASDAQ BUBBLE IN THE UNITED STATES 1995-2000

CHAPTER 14
THE SAVINGS AND LOANS CRISIS IN THE UNITED STATES

CHAPTER 15
CONCLUSION

"QUANTUM CRISIS II"
-THE GREAT FINANCIAL AND CREDIT CRISIS"
2007-2009

TABLE OF CONTENTS

PART 1– INTRODUCTION & BACKGROUND

PART 2 - THE REAL FINANCIAL & CREDIT CRISIS 2007-2009

CHAPTER 5

BACKGROUND OF PAST GLOBAL FINANCIAL CRISES

TYPES OF FINANCIAL CRISES

BANKING CRISES

SPECULATIVE BUBBLES AND CRASHES

INTERNATIONAL FINANCIAL CRISES

WIDER ECONOMIC CRISES

CAUSES AND CONSEQUENCES OF FINANCIAL CRISES

LEVERAGE

ASSET-LIABILITY MISMATCH

UNCERTAINTY AND HERD BEHAVIOR

REGULATORY FAILURES

FRAUD

CONTAGION

RECESSIONARY EFFECTS

THEORIES OF FINANCIAL CRISES

WORLD SYSTEMS THEORY

MINSKY'S THEORY

CO-ORDINATION GAMES

HERDING MODELS AND LEARNING MODELS

CHAPTER 6

TIMELINE OF GLOBAL FINANCIAL CRISIS OF 2007-2009

PRE-PANIC PHASE

PRELUDE TO PANIC PHASE

START OF THE FINANCIAL CRISIS

CHAPTER 7

THE REAL ESTATE BUBBLE & THE US SUB-PRIME CRISIS
HISTORICAL BACKGROUND
HOW DID THE CRISIS START?
THE HOUSING SECTOR CRISIS
RELATIONSHIP BETWEEN HOUSING CRISIS AND SUB-PRIME
SCANDAL
ETHICAL ISSUES

CHAPTER 8

FIRST MANIFESTATION OF STOCK/REAL ESTATE/BANKING BUBBLE
NORTHERN ROCK CRISIS IN THE UK
MORAL OF THE NORTHERN ROCK CRISIS
STOCK MARKET BUBBLE IN THE US
ASIA AND THE DECOUPLING THEORY
LOSSES IN ASIAN STOCKMARKET

CHAPTER 9

THE COLLAPSE OF BEAR STEARNS
BACKGROUND
FINANCIAL HISTORY
BEAR STEARNS FUNDS BAILOUT
GOVT. BAILOUT & SUBSEQUENT SALE TO JPMORGAN CHASE
MORAL BEHIND THIS REAL LIFE STORY
CHAPTER 10
COLLAPSE OF INDYMAC BANK
BACKGROUND
CAUSES OF INDYMAC BANK FAILURE
MORAL OF THE STORY

CHAPTER 11
THE LEHMAN BROTHERS FIASCO
BACKGROUND
CAUSES OF BANKRUPTCY
EFFECTS OF LEHMAN BANKRUPTCY
MORAL OF THE STORY

CHAPTER 12
CONTROVERSY BEHIND FREDDIE MAC AND FANNIE MAE
ORIGINS
ACCOUNTING ERRORS
GSE'S & THE GLOBAL FINANCIAL AND CREDIT CRISIS
MORAL OF THE STORY

CHAPTER 13
THE COLLAPSE OF WASHINGTON MUTUAL
BACKGROUND
HISTORY
ENTER THE SUB-PRIME MESS
EFFECTS OF CLOSURE
MORAL OF THE STORY

CHAPTER 14
**THE DEMISE OF THE INVESTMENT BANKING INDUSTRY
AND WALL STREET**
TARP (TROUBLED ASSET RELIEF PROGRAM) RECIPIENTS
USE OF TARP MONEY
MORGAN STANLEY AND THE GLOBAL CRISIS
GOLDMAN SACHS AND THE GLOBAL CRISIS
MORAL OF THE STORY

CHAPTER 17
THE BALANCE SHEET PROBLEMS AT MERRILL LYNCH
BACKGROUND
HISTORY
PROBLEMS AT MERRILL

CHAPTER 18
FINANCIAL PROBLEMS AT BANK OF AMERICA
BACKGROUND
ACQUISITION OF MERRILL LYNCH
MORAL OF STORY

CHAPTER 19
EUROPE AND THE BANKING CRISIS
BNP PARIBAS: INABILITY TO VALUE MORTGAGE RELATED ASSETS
SOCIETE GENERALE AND THE ROGUE TRADER
TROUBLE AT UK BANKS
CRISIS IN GERMANY
DUTCH AND BELGIAN BANKS IN TROUBLE
SWITZERLAND BANKING ISSUES
A SPECIAL CONGRATULATORY NOTE TO GORDON BROWN
BANKING CRISIS IN EASTERN EUROPE
MORAL OF THE STORY

CHAPTER 20
THE BOND RATING AGENCIES AND THEIR DEBACLE
IMPACT ON SUB-PRIME CRISIS
RATING ACTIONS DURING CRISIS
NEW GOVERNMENT REGULATIONS
MORAL OF THE STORY

CHAPTER 21
CREDIT DERIVATIVES
KEY UNFUNDED CREDIT DERIVATIVE PRODUCTS
CREDIT DEFAULT SWAP
TOTAL RETURN SWAP
KEY FUNDED CREDIT DERIVATIVE PRODUCTS
CREDIT LINKED NOTES
COLLATERIZED DEBT OBLIGATIONS (CDO's)
RISKS

CHAPTER 22
THE GREAT CREDIT CRISIS OF 2007-2009

CHAPTER 23
CRISIS IN THE INSURANCE INDUSTRY
BACKGROUND
THE FACTS
SITUATION IN THE US INSURANCE INDUSTRY
GENERAL EXPLANATIONS
MORAL OF THE STORY

CHAPTER 24

SUPER–CRISIS IN THE US INSURANCE INDUSTRY—THE FALL OF A GIANT (AIG)

BACKGROUND

HISTORY

AIG FINANCIAL PRODUCTS, LONDON

BAILOUT BY US GOVERNMENT

FURTHER LOSSES AT AIG

AIG AND FOREIGN BANK PAYOUTS

CHAPTER 24 (CONTINUED)

AIG & THE EMPLOYEE RETENTION BONUS ISSUE

FURTHER CONTRADICTIONS OF BONUS POOL

MORAL OF THE STORY

CHAPTER 25

BANKRUPTCY OF ICELAND

BACKGROUND

HISTORY

THE BANKING CRISIS

CAUSES OF BANKING CRISIS

LESSONS TO BE LEARNT FROM CRISIS

TIMELINE OF FINANCIAL CRISIS

MORAL OF STORY

CHAPTER 26

THE IMPACT OF FINANCIAL& CREDIT CRISIS ON AUSTRALASIA
THE INDIA SITUATION
INDIAN BANKING
NEGATIVE FALLOUT FROM CRISIS
CHINA AND THE GLOBAL CRISIS
FALLOUT FROM THE FINANCIAL AND CREDIT CRISIS
THE JAPANESE SCENARIO
JAPANESE ISSUES
HISTORY OF CRISIS
OVERALL EFFECT OF THE CRISIS
THE AUSTRALIAN SITUATION

CHAPTER 27

THE MADOFF PONZI SCANDAL IN THE UNITED STATES
BACKGROUND
CURRENT DEVELOPMENTS
BIGGER ISSUES

CHAPTER 28

THE STANFORD SCANDAL
BACKGROUND
RATE COMPARISON
RETALIATION BY EFFECTED COUNTRIES
SEC CASE
BIGGER ISSUES

CHAPTER 29

INTERNATIONAL RETALIATORY MOVES TO CONTAIN CRISIS

A SHORT HISTORY OF THE CRISIS

DEVELOPMENT AND CAUSATION

SEPTEMBER 2008 HAPPENINGS

GOVT. TAKEOVER OF HOME MORTGAGE LENDERS

MAJOR FINANCIAL FIRM FAILURE

MONEY MARKET FUNDS INSURANCE AND SHORT SALES PROHIBITIONS

SECTION 128

US TROUBLED ASSET RELIEF PROGRAM(TARP PROGRAM)

WEEK OF SEPTEMBER 21, 2008

WEEK OF SEPTEMBER 28,2008

KEY RISK INDICATORS IN SEPTEMBER 2008

REPORTS ON ECONOMIC ACTIVITY

EVENTS

BLUE MONDAY 2009 CRASH

GLOBAL RESPONSES TO FINANCIAL AND CREDIT CRISIS

ASIA PACIFIC RESPONSE

US RESPONSE

MARKET VOLATILITY WITHIN 401(k) AND US RETIREMENT PLANS

FEDERAL RESERVE OF THE US LOWERS INTEREST RATES

LEGISLATION

FEDERAL RESERVE RESPONSE

EUROPEAN UNION RESPONSE

POLITICAL EFFECTS AND PROJECTIONS RELATED TO THE ECONOMIC CRISIS

A SPECIAL NOTE ON US GOVERNMENT INITIATIVES

THE EMERGENCY ECONOMIC STABILIZATION ACT OF 2008

CHAPTER 29(CONTINUED)
INITIATIVES BY THE OBAMA ADMINISTRATION
NEW STIMULUS PLAN
DETAILS OF NEW STIMULUS PLAN
MAKING WORK PAY CREDIT
CHILD TAX CREDIT
AMERICAN OPPORTUNITY TAX CREDIT
ALTERNATIVE MINIMUM TAX (AMT)
OTHER PROVISIONS
THE AMERICAN RECOVERY AND REINVESTMENT ACT, 2009
COMPARISON OF HOUSE, SENATE & CONFERENCE
VERSIONS
CONFERENCE REPORT
PROVISIONS OF THE ACT

CONCLUSION

PART 3: WHAT WENT WRONG AND HOW TO FIX THE PROBLEM PERMANENTLY

CHAPTER 30
THE WORLD FINANCIAL SYSTEM EXPLAINED
BACKGROUND
FINANCIAL ARCHITECTURE
INTERNATIONAL INSTITUTIONS WHICH CONTROL THE GFS
GOVT. INSTITUTIONS WHO PLAY A ROLE IN THE GFS
PRIVATE PLAYERS IN THE GLOBAL FINANCIAL SYSTEM(GFS)
THE WASHINGTON CONSENSUS
WORLD TRADE v GLOBAL FINANCIAL SERVICES
THE FINANCIAL STABILITY FORUM

CHAPTER 31
COMPREHENSIVE UNDERSTANDING OF THE GLOBAL FINANCIAL CRISIS
BACKGROUND
TRANSFORMATION OF PROBLEM TO BANKING CRISIS
TRANSFORMATION OF BANKING CRISIS TO STOCK MARKET CRASH & CREDIT CRISIS
TRANFORMATION TO REAL ECONOMY DAMAGE
GLOBALIZATION OF FINANCIAL MARKETS
ISSUES

233

CHAPTER 35

PRACTICAL SOLUTIONS TO THE GREAT FINANCIAL AND CREDIT CRISIS

CHAPTER 36

POLICY RECOMMENDATIONS TO PREVENT ANY FUTURE CRISIS

CHAPTER 37

ITS NOT ALL ABOUT MONEY
MOVING AWAY FROM MATERIALISM
COMMUNITY AND SOCIAL RESPONSIBILITIES
LOVE & CARE INSIDE THE FAMILY UNIT
LOVE BEYOND THE FAMILY UNIT
A GLANCE AT GOOD HEALTH
PRAYER AND RELIGION
MEDITATION
PUTTING EVERYTHING TOGETHER TO LIVE BETTER

CHAPTER 38
CONCLUSION

"QUANTUM CRISIS 1
- THE ORIGIN OF GLOBAL FINANCIAL CRISES"
(29 USD-Free Shipping)

The first of a three-book series on the current Global Financial and Credit Crisis. This book provides a historical perspective on the major financial crises in the last four hundred years. In this journey, it weaves through difficult financial conditions in Asia, Europe and North America. It concludes with looking at the predominant causative strand running though such crises ---- the universal factors of greed and fear. It then provides some prescriptions in terms of how individuals can protect themselves in such dire conditions. A great starting book for anyone interested in understanding the current 2007–2009 global financial and credit crisis.

"QUANTUM CRISIS II
- The Great Financial and Credit Crisis 2007-2009"
(39 USD-Free shipping)

The second installment of the 3-book series entitled, "Quantum Crisis." This book starts its exposition with the beginnings of the global financial crisis, commencing in the Fall of 2007. It proceeds beautifully to sequentially elaborate on all significant developments of this crisis.

A special section deals with retaliatory steps taken by world governments to stem the crisis: it ends with the author's set of recommendations in terms of how to overcome this crisis effectively.

This book is a great read for anyone interested in:
(a) Understanding the current financial and credit crisis and
(b) Comprehending the investor challenge to save, grow and protect one's wealth in turbulent times.

"OFFSHORE INVESTMENTS –The Millionaire Vision." $99 USD(Free Shipping)

This book deals with the challenges of investing in offshore locations. It explains brilliantly the basic investment principles involved in saving, growing and protecting your capital. Then it deals with the advantages and drawbacks of world offshore centers. It continues with an understanding of trusts, foundations and other asset protection mechanisms. A must read for anyone planning to diversify his investment portfolio offshore!!!!!

"OFFSHORE HAVENS
-"The four best kept secrets of millionaires."
$99 USD(Free Shipping)

This book presents the top four offshore havens in the world in terms of the most important factors of superiority: privacy, safety, wealth management services and availability of professional expertise. The book then proceeds to explain the advantages/drawbacks of each of these top four centers. In the process it deals with current tax and investment legislation for international investments. This is a great book for international investors who seek advanced tax, investment and asset protection knowledge.

"YOU HAVE IT ALL-
Your Life is yours to truly discover and enjoy."
$29 USD(Free Shipping)

The author takes you through a marvelous journey, which ultimately questions the value of money in its relationship to Personal Happiness. Through his real Life experiences with his clients, the author discovered that Successful Living challenges one to achieve an optimal balance between Material pursuits and Happiness. He suggests means, methods and processes to live a more balanced and integrated Life leading to Wealth and Happiness simultaneously. A valuable book for anyone aspiring to Wealth and Happiness!!!!!

"QUANTUM SELLING"
$ 29 USD(Free Shipping)

This book deals with modern, practical and time-tested methods of achieving success in any Sales Endeavor. Through his business and sales experience of more than twenty years, culminating in achievement of all the top business awards in North America, the writer expounds a simple, time -proven technology of finding, growing and retaining clients in any field of business. This book is a must read for anyone desirous of building a successful Sales Practice/New business.

"QUANTUM SALES MANAGEMENT"
$ 29 USD(Free Shipping)

This publication focuses on proven success methods essential to the optimal management of a sales force. It discusses brilliant ideas addressing the four major challenges in professional sales management----- recruiting, training, developing and motivating salespeople. The research in this book is based on live studies and experiences of the author, who captured every major management award in North America, both at the corporate and professional body level in his field of financial service management. This book is extremely valuable to both new and experienced sales managers, who want to increase their sales numbers and achieve an even higher level of professional success.

"QUANTUM MARKETING"
How to create & grow profitable business opportunities
$ 29 USD(Free shipping)

This publication deals with the time-honored principles of marketing management. This book is truly unique in the sense that it approaches marketing from a 360 degree view. It does this by focusing on all aspects of marketing management, starting from the traditional 4 P's (Product, Price, Promotion and Place) to more elaborate concepts of the psychological, societal and philosophical implications of the marketing process. A must read for both marketing practitioners and enlightened marketing students, who want a deeper and significant understanding of the marketing process and their role in it.

"QUANTUM ETHICS"
$29 USD(Free shipping)

This book deals with some of the ethical concerns besetting the world today. It specifically discusses how major world corporations have ripped customers, investors and government authorities in their blind pursuit of money and fame. It throws a fresh light on some of the major world scandals and proposes ways and means of organizing, controlling and delivering a higher quality of ethical care to consumers. Through the process, it provides an understanding of the twin challenges of World Sustainability and Global Warming------these constitute two of the most important ethical considerations of our age. A great book for anyone interested in exploring how Ethics and Business clash and how to protect oneself from dishonesty, misrepresentation and poor business practice.

"QUANTUM PUBLIC SPEAKING"
How to Influence People through Superlative Communication(29 USD-Free Shipping)

Here, for once, is a fresh and entertaining book on Effective Public Speaking. The author has shared his twenty plus years of experience as a major public speaker, debater and trainer of sales people. This brilliant and enjoyable book discusses how anyone can master Public Speaking through one-on-one communication and in group public speaking. A must read for anyone who wants to increase his communication power with a view to positively influencing people!!!!!

**BOOKS CAN BE ORDERED DIRECTLY AT:
www.pioneer-communication.com or at
rdrajpal@yahoo.com**

10% DISCOUNT FOR 2–3 BOOKS
15% DISCOUNT FOR 4–5 BOOKS
20% DISCOUNT FOR 6–7 BOOKS
25% DISCOUNT FOR MORE THAN 7 BOOKS

**** NOTE ALL BOOKS MUST BE ORDERED AT
THE SAME TIME FOR DISCOUNT TO APPLY
FREE SHIPPING AND DISCOUNTS ONLY PROVIDED WHEN
ORDERS PLACED DIRECTLY AT ABOVE WEBSITE
FREE SHIPPING APPLIES ONLY TO CONTINENTAL UNITED
STATES DELIVERY